Charles E. Booth is a synonym
His preaching is filled with an
their current circumstances into the presence of God. His preaching impacts
and inspires audiences all around the world. His powerful sermon delivery
consistently persuades people to believe in the power of God's grace and mercy.

Wayne G. Thompson
Senior Pastor, First Baptist Institutional Church, St. Petersburg, Florida

I thank God for Dr. Charles Booth and his new book, *Stronger in My Broken Places.* You can be assured that this book is from his personal experience. He has had a "wonderful time" while in the storms of his life.

Bishop Jerome H. Ross, Sr.
Triedstone Baptist Church/Kingdom Connection Fellowship International,
Columbus, Ohio

Dr. Charles E. Booth has pulled together some of his most powerful and life-enhancing sermons to help followers of Christ gain strength, direction, and encouragement during these challenging times. This is a must-read for any person of any age or background.

Dr. Jasmin "Dr. Jazz" Scularck
Senior Pastor, City of Jericho, Landover, Maryland

In these insightful sermons the Rev. Dr. Charles E. Booth, one of the great pulpit voices of our generation, again demonstrates the power of the sermon and of the spoken word to transform lives, to meet people where they are, and to help both reader and listener see God more clearly in a world bent on drowning out God's voice. Whenever I listen to Charles Booth or read his sermon masterpieces, I am convinced that good preaching is alive and well.

Rev. Dr. J. Wendell Mapson, Jr.
Pastor, Monumental Baptist Church, Philadelphia, Pennsylvania

Charles Edward Booth is one of the premier preachers of this or any day. This compilation of sermons/messages shows why. Biblical, practical, pastoral—this book is a *must*-read for broken people!

Bishop Timothy J. Clarke
Senior Pastor, First Church of God, Columbus, Ohio

For 25 years I have been a fan of the preaching of the Rev. Dr. Charles E. Booth. His anointed ability to open the scriptures and bring to light the truth of God and the love of God as revealed in Jesus Christ has enabled and empowered countless persons including myself to move forth courageously ahead in life knowing that we are more than conquerors. I commend this book of sermons to people who are already disciples of Christ and those yet to be. It is the biblical, powerful, and practical preaching that this book exhibits that gives men and women reason to live and to find strength in their broken places!

Kenneth D.R. Clayton
Senior Pastor, St. Luke Baptist Church, Paterson, New Jersey

Some of the most spiritual encounters that I've relished in my life have been sitting at the feet of Dr. Charles E. Booth and the delivery of his sermons. Those encounters have challenged me, encouraged me, and literally amazed me. The writings of Dr. Booth accomplish the same but in a different way. He writes with a melody, a challenge, and a solution all at the same time. This book is a spiritual experience for transformation and overcoming the obstacles of life.

Dr. Harold A. Hudson
Associate Dean of Doctoral Studies, United Theological Seminary, Dayton, Ohio

Stronger in My Broken Places: Claiming a Life of Fullness in God is an instant classic. Whether I am reading his writing or listening to Dr. Booth teach or preach in person, what God does through Dr. Charles E. Booth is always enriching and impactful. I know this book of sermons will be stimulating to your mind, exciting to your heart, and uplifting to your soul. I highly recommend every Christian to add this publication to their library as soon as possible.

Rev. Dr. Harry L. White, Jr.
Pastor, Watts Chapel Missionary Baptist Church, Raleigh, North Carolina

STRONGER
—IN MY—
Broken
PLACES
Claiming a Life of
Fullness in God

DR. CHARLES E. BOOTH
Foreword by William H. Curtis

Published by MMGI Books, Chicago, IL 60636

www.mmgibooks.com

Stronger in My Broken Places:
Claiming a Life of Fullness in God

Library of Congress Cataloging-in-Publication Data

Stronger in My Broken Places: Claiming a Life of Fullness in God by Charles E. Booth

p. cm

ISBN 978-1-939774-13-2 (pbk. : alk. paper)

Religious life. 2. Women and Men – Conduct of life. 3. Christian – Development.

Booth, Charles E.

Printed in the U.S.A.

CONTENTS

This book is dedicated to the faithful disciples whom
I sought to serve for the last 36 years at the
Mount Olivet Baptist Church of Columbus, Ohio.

I acknowledge the following persons who were instrumental
in the completion of this book for publication:
Reverend Darryl D. Sims,
Mrs. Carol Bates Gardner,
Dr. Betty Lovelace-Ross,
Dr. William H. Curtis,
and the amazing MMGI Books
team of consultants.

FOREWORD

In recent years, I have soberly accepted middle-age status and, along with that, a mentoring position in the lives of many pastors. To this task I attempt to be honest and committed, which necessitates that I answer, among the many questions that are asked of me, the following: Who are your favorite preachers and, of them, who speaks clearest to you in helping to shape your homiletic? Who represents an enduring model of sermonic freshness and pulpit relevancy? I am always eager to share, after mentioning my own Pastor, Bishop Walter S. Thomas, a name that is on every list in my life regardless of the question: Dr. Charles E. Booth.

I first heard Dr. Booth in November 1982, and I have remained passionately and energetically connected to his preaching and ministry ever since. The content, integrity, prophetic commitment, and pulpit passion I was introduced to so many years ago has impressively continued to grow, mature, and become perfected by a man who has given his life to preaching ministry.

I believe that life experiences give the call of ministry in our lives its lift and authority. Dr. Booth has been a voice for those who find themselves living in the gaps of life; and what one senses is that they are listening to a fellow traveler who is well-acquainted with the rippling undercurrents that are pushing us in so many spiritual and emotional directions. Dr. Booth incarnates what it means to allow God to demonstrate His grace in our broken places. The loss of an eye in his youth, a devastating fire that almost destroyed his home, the fight against cancer, and other private battles that we all must face have shaped Dr. Booth's hermeneutic and made him believable when he stands. Yet, when he stands, it becomes clear that these experiences have been enveloped and interpreted in a love relationship he has with Jesus that allows him to find the note of redemption and salvation even from these experiences. Indeed, he is the example of living stronger in the broken places. You will find him historically accurate in his interpretation of scripture, passionately prophetic about God's demand for justice and liberation, and futuristically hopeful that God's Kingdom can be manifested on the earth.

Rev. Dr. William H. Curtis
Senior Pastor, Mount Ararat Baptist Church
Pittsburgh, Pennsylvania

MAKING THE BEST OUT OF A BAD SITUATION

Jephthah the Gileadite was a mighty warrior. His father was Gilead; his mother was a prostitute. Gilead's wife also bore him sons, and when they were grown up, they drove Jephthah away. "You are not going to get any inheritance in our family," they said, "because you are the son of another woman." So Jephthah fled from his brothers and settled in the land of Tob, where a group of adventurers gathered around him and followed him. Some time later, when the Ammonites made war on Israel, the elders of Gilead went to get Jephthah from the land of Tob. "Come," they said, "be our commander, so we can fight the Ammonites." Jephthah said to them, "Didn't you hate me and drive me from my father's house? Why do you come to me now, when you're in trouble?" **Judges 11:1-7, NIV**

I want to preach today about making the best out of a bad situation. In Charles Dickens' *A Tale of Two Cities*, there was this opening line that is quite memorable: "It was the best of times, it was the worst of times." When I think about those words written well over 100 years ago, I think that they are most appropriate for the times in which we live now in these dawning years of the 21st Century.

In many ways, these are the best of times. They are the best of times in terms of technological achievement. We have at our fingertips now appliances that make life so easy. We drive automobiles today that 100 years ago were almost unthinkable. There are so many things that the wonders of technology have placed upon us that, in so many ways, make life more convenient.

Man is a genius. Man has creative ability. Out of the thoughts of men and women have come wonderful things. But the same brain that can create positive and constructive things is the same brain that can create that which is destructive. So Dickens is right. These are the best of times, but they are also the worst of times, for the genius of humankind can also bring about what we call greed.

It is the greed of humankind that places the whole world in a global mess. Economic markets worldwide are in a tailspin. The great question that looms today in the minds of people north, south, east, and west is how will we come out of this economic crunch? The problem is not so much economics as it is how will the human mind finally come to the realization that it cannot be selfish and have civilization survive?

How and when will we realize that to continue being selfish, to continue being greedy, means that civilization as we know it will no longer survive? Unemployment is unbelievable. Health care is still beyond the reach of millions. We shuddered when Chrysler went into bankruptcy, and then General Motors followed suit. These are the best of times, but they are also the worst of times. And because we are living in the worst of times, there are many of us who cannot cope with these bad times, and they commit suicide.

Suicide is the ultimate answer to those who believe they have no hope. And there are people who cannot cope who don't commit suicide, but who become chemically dependent because they need some kind of substance to help them deal with life's vicissitudes. It doesn't matter whether you are saint or a sinner, whether you are in the church or out; the worst of times affects all of us. For those of you who have come into the body of Christ believing that somehow this is a hiding place, yes, in one sense it is that; but you shouldn't come to the church to hide from life's realities. You should come to the church because you want God to give you strength to face life's vicissitudes, and more than that, God gives you strength to overcome life's realities.

We don't really say this with power anymore, and we ought to, but if you are a child of God, you ought to be able to say "I can do all things...." *All things.* I don't care how difficult it gets, I don't care how dark life becomes, I can do all things through Jesus Christ who strengthens me. In fact, the beauty of our faith is that the darker life gets, the brighter Christ becomes. The more difficult the times are, the more real He is. I can do all things through Jesus Christ who strengthens me. Let man continue in his greed. Let Wall Street require a bailout. Let the automobile industry go to pot. But when it's all said and done, when the smoke finally clears, and the dust settles, I will stand because Christ is Alpha and Omega, the Beginning and the End, the First and the Last. So with Christ standing in the worst of times, who will be right by his side, declaring that the Lord will make a way anyhow?

The Bible says in this 11th chapter of Judges that there was a Gileadite whose name was Jephthah. He was a lesser-known judge. The first introduction that we have to him or about him is that he was a mighty warrior. His father, Gilead, was a man of economic means, a married man who had many sons. Jephthah comes into play because Gilead, his father, steps outside of his marriage, has a relationship with a prostitute, and produces a son. Jephthah is the product of his father's passion and his mother's profession. His brothers despise him. When Gilead dies, this is the opportune occasion for the brothers to tell Jephthah what they really think of him. When the reading of the will comes, they tell him it's time now for him to exit. We've tolerated you all these years. You have represented an embarrassment to all of us, and you shall not have one part or parcel to our father's inheritance. Get out! The mother seemingly does not come to his defense. Not one of the elders comes to his defense. Not one of his brothers comes to his defense, and he leaves the family compound to march out into life, if you will, as a soldier of fortune.

When next we pick up the story, we are told that Jephthah finds himself among a group of adventurers who are looking for somebody to lead them. This young man becomes their leader because in him they see leadership ability. Now the question that I want to raise is how did he become a leader? He has been rejected by family and by the community, and he has no real support system. Yet, he does the unthinkable: he makes something out of his life. There is no indication in the text that he became chemically dependent because nobody supported him. The text does not say that he threw a pity party because nobody liked him. He does not immerse himself in a temper tantrum. He does not begin blaming the circumstances of his birth for what he can become.

Not one of us has been born with a silver spoon in his or her mouth, and even if you are born with a silver spoon, you're still going to have trials, struggles, tribulations, and temptations. In other words, you will find yourself, time and time again, in the middle of a bad situation. The question that looms this before us is how do I make the best out of it?

God does not want those of us who claim Him to be chronic complainers. I think that some of us get on God's nerves. But because He's so loving, gracious and merciful, He tolerates us and puts up with our foolishness. Now, God told us we would have difficulties. He told us we would climb the rough side of the mountain. He told us that folk will turn on us. Our problem is we didn't take God seriously and now that we are between a rock and a hard place, we seemingly have forgotten what God told us. "If I told you there would be a difficult time," God says, "have enough faith to believe that I have enough provision for you to make the best out of every bad situation."

What a word, particularly during this season when our young people are graduating and when they are looking towards brighter horizons. What a word for those of us who are adults and who wonder how much more can we take.

Jephthah makes the best of out a bad situation. First, he does not take responsibility for something over which he has absolutely no control. Jephthah says, "I will not live in the captivity of self-harassment. I will not hold myself bondage in guilt that I don't deserve. I have nothing to do with my father's passion. I have nothing to do with my mother's profession. I didn't tell my father to step outside of the boundaries of his marriage and have a relationship with a prostitute. I was not behind the closed doors. But even though I was not behind the closed doors, I was still in the mind of God. Even though I've become the product of my father's passion and my mother's profession, somewhere in the great mind of God, He conceptualized me and knew that I would be born in a bad situation, so He began to chart my destiny so that I might make the best out of it. But I will not take responsibility for anything that is beyond my control."

Somebody is living today in the tomb of guilt because you are harassing yourself over something that you have no control over. It's not just about a boy being born to a prostitute and to a father who went beyond the boundaries of marriage. The issue is bigger than that. How many are beating themselves up because they have no job? Perhaps you were fired or terminated, or let go. One has no control over that. How many are beating themselves up over issues that go back generations?

You know my story. I'm transparent about it. I'm not ashamed of it. You know about how my father walked out on my mother, and my mother was forced to live and to raise two children basically on her own, but those are not excuses for me not making something out of myself with the help of Almighty God. So what if your birth father was not around? So what if, like mine, your stepfather was an alcoholic? You have another father. Your birth daddy may not be there, and your step-daddy may not be what he ought to be, but our Heavenly Father watches over us. My Daddy is your Daddy. He's the Daddy of black people, white people, red people, yellow people, poor people, middle-class people, upper-class people, rich people, and no-class people.

My Father is the richest Being in all of creation, and that makes me a prince. Not a bastard because you're born outside of a marriage, but a prince. Not because you're born on the wrong side of the family, but a prince. Even though you come out of the hood, you are a prince because your Father is a king. Young lady, you are a princess because your Father is a king.

People, in general, and African American people, in particular, need to understand that we must stop having guilt feelings over issues beyond our control. I'm not going to let racism keep me down. I did not cause slavery or racism, but I do bear responsibility for making something out of myself.

Jephthah, whose name means "the Lord has opened the womb," grew up with no support from his family or his community; yet, he grew to become a mighty warrior. Whence came his positive outlook? Where did he get his constructive worldview? He learned to block out what his family thought of him and what friends thought of him as well as what the community thought of him. He began to think about what *God* thought of him! Jephthah must have come to conclude that if he came out of his mother's womb, God must have purpose for his life. He riveted his understanding on divine purpose and not on family understanding.

The fact that I am born, the fact that I'm alive, the fact that I live, move, and have my being shows that I have promise, potential, and possibilities.

All of us are unique, are we not? There are no two people who are exactly alike in the world. Our uniqueness sometimes creates the problem. Sometimes our uniqueness creates enemies. I'm convinced that this is not just an issue of Jephthah being born out of wedlock. That's just a part of the story. The other part of the story must be that in his growth and development, his brothers saw in him what they didn't see in themselves—that with all this negativity around him, the boy still had a positive attitude as well as a sense of somebody-ness.

They've done everything they could to destroy him, but instead of getting weaker, Jephthah grew stronger, and they saw that he was in possession of a psychology, a way of thinking, that they didn't possess. He possessed a philosophy and a way of life that they did not. He had a spirituality they themselves did not possess. Sometimes one is despised, disliked and hated because of one's uniqueness, but one ought to adopt a sense of "I can't help it": "I can't help it that God loves me anyhow. I can't help it that, despite my circumstance, God still blesses me. And I'm not going to allow your inability to accept my uniqueness as reason for me not to become who I have been conceptualized in God's mind to be. It must come to pass. Whether you put obstacles in my pathway or not,

I must become what my destiny decrees because I'm not responsible for that which is beyond my control."

Recently, I listened to the wonderful speech that President Obama made outside of Buchenwald in Germany, the concentration camp where thousands of Jews were gassed to death. I remember several years ago when I was in Germany visiting the concentration camp at Dachau. I remember standing there, looking at the crematorium and wondering how could anyone be so inhumane? What was it in the background of Adolf Hitler that created such hatred for the Jewish people?

All racism, at its root, is a hatred of another's uniqueness. There are people who hate and despise others, simply because they are different. Well, that's what life is. Life is about differences. Life is about diversity, but my difference does not give one reason to dislike me. But it was not President Barack Obama who captured my attention. It was the little Jewish man who spoke after him, the 1986 Nobel Peace Prize laureate, the holocaust survivor, Elie Wiesel. There was a line that grabbed me. He said, "My otherness is what others don't like. My uniqueness is my otherness. Wouldn't life be a boring enterprise if all of us looked the same, talked the same, thought the same? My God, I love me, but I wouldn't want a world full of me, and you're a fool if you think you want a world full of you, because there are times when I don't like me. Thank God there are other folk in the world!"

I applaud the uniqueness of others. I don't want to be insecure when it comes to somebody's otherness. My otherness is my uniqueness, and my uniqueness is what makes me. Therefore, celebrate my otherness. Don't become jealous of it.

There's only one Being who is jealous but never insecure: God. God says, "I am a jealous God. I will have no other gods before me." Just because God is jealous does not mean that He's insecure. He can't be insecure. How is He going to be insecure when the earth is the Lord's and the fullness thereof"? He says, "I am jealous when you put everybody and everything before me when it's you that I made, and everything you have is because of my grace, my love, and my mercy. I'm jealous, but I'm never insecure. I can't be insecure because I'm God all by myself." Aren't you glad He's God all by Himself?

Look at what else we see in Jephthah, this mighty warrior from Gilead. He makes something out of himself because he recognizes that strength comes from within and not from without. He did not wait for support and validation outside of himself, and his success in life was not dependent on outside support. Sometimes one must learn like David to encourage one's self. Family and friends won't always be supportive. Nor will the community always be in one's corner. When support does not come from without, one must get inspiration and encouragement from within. One can't live waiting for people always to support one's efforts.

Remember when David and his mighty men came forth from the battle, and they came to the city of refuge where David, with his men, their wives, and their children made habitation? They discovered that the enemy had come and ravaged the city, burned it to the ground. All of the women and the children were taken away. The text says in 2 Samuel, that the men who had been so loyal to David were ready to stone him because they blamed him for the capture of their wives and children. But when they sought to stone him, the Bible says, "David encouraged himself."

Now, in order to encourage yourself, one must have an understanding of God. One can't encourage what isn't there. One must have something on the inside that says, "If God is for me, that's better than the entire world against me."

God is calling for Christians to be spiritual amphibians. An amphibian has both lungs and gills, so that when things get bad on land, it can leave the surface, shut down its lungs, open up its gills, and go down into the water and live beyond the sight of the enemy. God is calling us to be spiritual amphibians. He's telling us to live in the world, but when the world gets rough, go inside of one's self and suck up the energy that comes from God, energy that says, "They who wait upon the Lord shall renew their strength...." Energy that says, "Greater is He that is in me than he that is in the world." Energy that says, "No weapon formed against me shall be able to prosper."

Too many of us are not amphibious. We only know how to live in one realm, but one must learn how to live in two different worlds. One must learn when to tuck in one's lungs and let out one's spiritual gills and get down into the waters of one's interior and come up stronger than ever before. Is there anybody who is a living embodiment of the fact that when you tuck yourself in and fence the world out and get power from God, you can handle whatever the world throws at you?

One does not need drugs, liquor, or sex. However, one does need God. Are there any testimonies that God makes the difference? How many know what it is to dwell in the secret place where it's just you and God? There is power in your secret place. There is an anointing.

The next time somebody hurts your feelings, say, "All right, I've got to leave you now. I've got to go to my secret place. I'm letting in my lungs, and I'm letting down my spiritual gills, but I'll be back. You just wait for me, and when I get back, I'll be ready for you because my power is not from without. My power comes from within."

Jephthah takes no responsibility for that over which he has no control, and he finds inspiration within and not without. All of this he does as a boy, as a child who grows into manhood, which makes the third point logical: In order for one not to take responsibility for that over which one has no control, and if, in times of difficulty, one is going to draw one's inspiration from within and without, one must have a goal. There must be some objective, some future to which God is pushing you, driving you. A lot of us don't understand what it means to be pushed and don't know what it is to be driven. I am pushed to do what I do. I'm driven to do what I do, and anybody who lives under the auspices of God's Spirit knows that you don't operate under your own command; you are pushed and driven by God.

Jephthah says, "I have a future. Kick me out of the family. Write me out of the will, but I still have a future." Jephthah had a future. His family and friends tried to rewrite his script. The community tried to rewrite his script, but he stayed on point. And watch this: The text says that when they kicked him out, he didn't argue with them. Jephthah developed his leadership appeal so that immediately, God raised up some folk who needed what he had to offer. Whenever somebody kicks you out, that's when God kicks in. Being kicked out might be the end of a chapter, but the book isn't complete, and to be kicked out of one chapter is God's way of saying, "I'm getting ready to kick you into another."

Do you know what it is to live in expectation, to live in hope? When I come out of the secret place, I'm looking for my next blessing. I'm looking for God to open the next door. I'm waiting for God to make a new way.

The text says there were a group of adventurers, which really means a group of men who are empty. They are thieves, robbers, idle and reckless men. They rob, and steal, and kill. And all of a sudden, there appears before them this young man from Gilead, who immediately is perceived as somebody with leadership qualities, and they followed him.

All those years of rejection, all those years of family and communal hatred, produced a young man who knew what it was to draw encouragement from within, and who also knew that God had a future for him. God put this mighty warrior in the midst of a bunch of idle, empty, reckless men who needed somebody to set them on the right path, and Jephthah comes to prominence. The elders who come from Gilead hear about it and go to him. If you stick with God and allow Him to rewrite your script, the very folk who kicked you out will try to get you back.

Listen to what Jephthah says, "Aren't you the ones who kicked me out?" However, he doesn't make them beg because he understands what Mordecai meant when he said to Esther, "Who knows but that you have come to royal position for such a time as this?" (Esther 4:14, NIV). When your enemies come back, don't get up on your high horse. Don't try to rub dirt in their faces. Remember, God rewrote the script so that you could actualize what He had already conceptualized. And Jephthah goes to God and asks God for strength to give leadership so that he can lead his people against the Ammonites.

When I think about Jephthah, I think about another man. They kicked Him out, too. They didn't like Him. He was born of a virgin, but they didn't really believe it, and He came out of a no-man's land called Nazareth. Before that, He left his father's home, came down through forty and two generations, tiptoed through the back door of human history, gestated in the womb of a virgin, and nine months later dropped from her loins on a bed of straw in Bethlehem's manger. They brought Him gifts of gold, frankincense, and myrrh. Heaven came down and glory filled our souls.

Christmas comes every day, because when He came down, He came down to find somebody empty like me, idle like me, reckless like me, foolish like me, and guess what? Somebody like you, too!

Aren't you glad that God sent His Son in the midst of your emptiness, idleness, and recklessness to lift us up and take us to where God wants you?

I came to Him empty. I came to Him idle. I came to Him reckless, and guess what I found? I found in Him a resting place, and He has made me glad.

Do I have any resting place people? Do I have anybody who is glad that He found you in your idleness; that He found you in your emptiness; that He found you in your recklessness? Aren't you glad that when you were on your way to hell, no heaven in sight, no God to glorify, too mean to live and not yet ready to die, God sent His Son? I thank God that on my journey I heard a voice, I saw a light, I felt a spirit that picked me up and turned me around.

I am thanking God today that however dark it might be, I've got some good news. There's a bright side somewhere. Whatever you ask in Jesus' name will close the gap between yesterday and today, which is why we're in church and down on our knees because God hears and answers prayer.

It's bad, but I'm not throwing in the towel. I've got a future. Whenever life shuts one door, I have the confidence that God is getting ready to open another door. What He's about to open is better than what's been.

Encourage yourself because you have a future. It's a bright future. It's a beautiful future. It's a brandishing future. It's a brilliant future. These are the worst of times, but they are also the best of times.

GETTING OUT OF MOAB

Now it came to pass, in the days when the judges ruled, that there was a famine in the land. And a certain man of Bethlehem, Judah, went to dwell in the country of Moab, he and his wife and his two sons. The name of the man was Elimelech, the name of his wife was Naomi, and the names of his two sons were Mahlon and Chilion—Ephrathites of Bethlehem, Judah. And they went to the country of Moab and remained there. Then Elimelech, Naomi's husband, died; and she was left, and her two sons. Now they took wives of the women of Moab: the name of the one was Orpah, and the name of the other Ruth. And they dwelt there about ten years. Then both Mahlon and Chilion also died; so the woman survived her two sons and her husband. Then she arose with her daughters-in-law that she might return from the country of Moab, for she had heard in the country of Moab that the Lord had visited His people by giving them bread. . . . Now the two of them went until they came to Bethlehem. And it happened, when they had come to Bethlehem, that all the city was excited because of them; and the women said, "Is this Naomi?" But she said to them, "Do not call me Naomi; call me Mara, for the Almighty has dealt very bitterly with me. I went out full, and the Lord has brought me home again empty. Why do you call me Naomi, since the Lord has testified against me, and the Almighty has afflicted me?"

Ruth 1:1-6, 19-21, NKJV

At the writing of the text, ancient Israel was in the midst of dark and evil times. It was the time when Judah and Israel did very much as they pleased. The judges were men and women, sandwiched between the patriarchs and prophets, who gave direction and leadership to God's people. Perhaps more than any other verse in the book of Judges, one

verse that speaks to us with clarion certainty is the verse that says, "...
in the time of the Judges every man and woman sat beneath his or her
own vine and fig tree and did as he or she pleased."

In many ways, I think that this can be said of the day and time in
which we live—we are living in a day and time when people sit beneath
their own spiritual and ethical vine and fig tree and pretty much do
as they please. There does not seem to be anymore a definitive right
or wrong. We are living in a day of moral and ethical laxity. We live
in a day when for many our ethics are defined by the situation. In this
postmodern era, everything is relative. It appears that we have come to
a day and time where there are no absolutes.

But I rise today to say that all things are not relative; we do not have
the right to think and choose pretty much as we want. We do in the
sense that we are creatures of free will, but once we become saved,
once we become men and women in Christ, we submit to Him and He
becomes the Way, the Truth, and the Life.

So in the text we see that there is a famine. The Law identifies famine
as one of the judgments God will bring on His people when they are
unfaithful (Deuteronomy 28:23-24). Given the spiritual climate of the
times, it is clear that the family of Elimelech fled during a time when
most in the area had turned to Baal worship.

From a logical point of view, one can understand the rationale on the
part of Elimelech to leave Judah and go to Moab. In Moab, Elimelech
and his family would be able to make a living, food would be plentiful,
and they would be allowed to practice their religion. However, there is
a question to be raised: Did Elimelech go to Moab on faith or unbelief?
Do not forget that Moab is a stench in the nostrils of God. Elimelech's
name means "My God Is King." According to Deuteronomy, if the

people would repent, Yahweh would withdraw His anger and lift the famine. It seems, however, that Elimelech designed his own solution—run to Moab—instead of calling on God for mercy and repenting of the sins that plagued the nation of Judah during the dark days of the judges. If Elimelech truly lived out the meaning of his name, it seems to me he would have been a man of prayer who would plead to the holy presence for the Lord to lift the famine. Instead, he takes his family to a land that is a spiritual "garbage can" in the sight of God. While it was his intent to "sojourn" in the land of Moab—not live there, but wait out the famine and return to Bethlehem when it was over—the reality is that Elimelech and his family stayed in Moab for ten years. And it is during this period of time that he and his sons die.

And consequently, Naomi and her two daughters-in-law are stuck in Moab. Naomi is stuck in a foreign and alien land. She is stuck where the people worship CHEMOSH, the foreign god who required human sacrifice. She is stuck in Moab where King Eglon had pressured Israel into servitude for 18 years.

Have you ever gotten stuck in Moab? Moab is any place, relationship, or state of mind where God is absent. Moab is the place where you know God would frown upon certain behavior. Moab is any relationship where God is not the centerpiece. Moab is any state of mind where ugly, wicked, evil, and violent thoughts abound. All of us have been to Moab. Some of us are mentally in Moab today. Some of us were in Moab last night. Moab is the place where you stayed longer than you intended to stay and paid a price you never intended to pay.

How do you get out of Moab?

Leaving Moab requires serious decision making. One gets out of Moab by realizing the impact and influence of assimilation. We know the expression "association brings on assimilation." When Elimelech brought his family into the land of Moab, he brought them among a people who represented a syncretistic society. To syncretize means to combine or fuse different beliefs or practices. There Jews would be allowed to practice their faith, but they would do so in a culture that was paganistic and idolatrous. The reason for the famine in Judah— the place Elimelech's family had left—was because the people had syncretized their faith and worshipped Baal.

So often we feel that we can associate with people who are not Christians and be around calamities that we know God does not like with the belief that we are immune and untouchable. When you play with fire, you will get burned!

So while in Moab, Naomi's sons, Mahlon and Chilion, married women from Moab. These young men assimilated into the culture. The text says, "They lifted their wives, they carried their wives," which comes down to this: They abducted their wives. They had been away from Judah. They had been away from Bethlehem for so long that they had forgotten what it meant to really court a woman and to take a woman as a bride. They abducted Orpah and Ruth. The inference is that these young men who were not rogues before they left Bethlehem, who were not guilty perhaps of domestic violence before they left Bethlehem, had become so assimilated into the culture by their association that they abduct these women and make them marry them. The mystery is how Orpah and Ruth turned out to be such good women when they were married to such hellish men.

Mahlon and Chilion weren't like that when they got into Moab. You've got to watch where you take your children. You must watch what you expose your children to because you don't know what exposure will put in their mindset that is contrary to God. The Black community has not always been a community of Bloods and Crips. The Black community has not always been a community where chemical dependency and drug addictions have flourished. That stuff came from Moab. We've got sons and daughters who are pot smokers because their mothers and fathers were pot smokers. We've got sons and daughters who are alcoholics because their mothers and fathers were liquor heads. We've got sons and daughters who will cuss out the preacher and anybody else because they listen to profanity every day, because home for them is Moab. One of the reasons we cannot control our children in the community and in the school is because they have become uncontrollable at home, Moab.

Everybody knows that I love The Temptations. You may remember— or remember seeing in the movie—that sad part about Paul Williams, the one whom they considered to be the soul of the group. He and Eddie Kendricks had come out of the church in the south. It is said that Paul Williams never drank anything stronger than milk until he started hanging out in Moab. When The Temptations started making a name for themselves and their lives jumped in the fast lane, this man who never drank anything stronger than milk became an alcoholic and engaged in abusive behavior towards his wife. In the end, he was the first Temptation to die by putting a bullet to his head and taking his own life.

Moab will destroy you! Your associations will bring about an assimilation, a fusion, a blend that you don't want. Just because it's on television doesn't mean it's right. Just because everybody's doing it does not mean it's right. Get the hell out of Moab before the hell of Moab destroys you! How many of you have been in Moab and discovered that there are behaviors you started engaging in that were not a part of who you are?

Assimilation can be quick, but, more often than not, it is subtle. We become captivated by the culture in a slow process. Few are like Daniel, Hananiah, Mishael, and Azariah, who refused to eat the king's meat and be assimilated into Babylonian culture. All of us know people whose initial journey began with the best of intentions, but somewhere along the way they became assimilated. Moab also appears in the church. We drag a corporate mindset into the church! We want to syncretize the faith with all of this new age, cross-less Christianity. Keep Moab out of the church! To get out of Moab you need to realize that association brings on assimilation.

Secondly, one gets out of Moab by coming to the realization that one doesn't have to live in another's mistaken judgment. Elimelech was dead. Naomi was now a widow. Elimelech had made a mistake bringing his family to Moab, but his mistake did not necessitate Naomi's continuation in that mistake. She was faithful and committed to her husband. While she may not have desired to go to Moab, Naomi respected her husband enough to follow him because he was the head of their household. But after 10 years it became crystal clear to Naomi that leaving Judah had been an error. When her husband died and then her two sons, Naomi was alienated. She depended upon her husband and then her sons for support. Now all three were gone. When they died, Naomi said, "I'm not living in my husband's mistake any longer. I recognize that he made a mistake, and I shall not live in his mistaken judgment any longer."

There is a point in everyone's life where you bear the responsibility for your own decisions. Just because you love somebody doesn't mean you follow them blindly. There comes a moment when you've got to determine whether or not somebody's decision reflects God. Just because they died in Moab doesn't mean I have to.

Do you remember Madeline Murray O'Hare? It took her eight years to appeal to the Supreme Court, and because of Madeline Murray O'Hare, we now don't have prayer in our schools. The one she marched before the Supreme Court was her son, William. He was a little boy saturated with his mother's atheistic philosophy. A little boy greatly impacted and influenced, he didn't know what he believed at that point, but his mother put him up before the Supreme Court and said that she didn't want her son to be told that he had to read the Judeo-Christian scriptures and that he had to pray in the classroom. Because of that, the Supreme Court struck down Bible reading and prayer in public schools.

When William got older and happened to go by somebody's church, he heard about and accepted Jesus Christ. There's power in this Gospel. I don't know who the preacher was, but one day William heard the Gospel and decided that he was no longer going to walk in his mother's mistaken judgment. He heard the voice of Jesus say, "Come unto me and rest, lay down thy weary one, lay down thy head upon my breast." And that's not just William's testimony. That's mine, and it ought to be yours as well. I came to Jesus just as I was.

I know others who came just as they were, too. You were messed up, screwed up. You were weary, worn, and sad. He made you glad, and that's why you can go to Moab and work every day and still keep your sanity. That's why God can keep you in that marriage or that relationship or keep your mind settled when your children are driving you crazy, because you found in Him a resting place, and He has made you glad.

If you're going to get out of Moab, you have to realize that your associations bring about assimilation. If you're going to get out of Moab, you have to learn not to live in somebody else's mistaken judgment. Finally, if you're going to get out of Moab, you have to keep in touch with someone in Bethlehem. Even though she was in Moab, Naomi still had ties to Bethlehem. By keeping in touch with Bethlehem, Naomi was told that the famine had been lifted. There was bread and fertility again in Palestine.

Even if sojourning in Moab, one must keep in touch with those who have "the bread." The Moab crowd had no bread. There are those of us who never cut off those who live in Bethlehem. Never forget where the bread is. Naomi needed the bread because Moab and the death of her husband and sons left her empty. Her disposition had changed. She changed her name from Naomi—"pleasant"—to Mara—"bitter." Life in Moab had made her bitter.

You've been in Moab so long that Moab has zapped your energy, zapped your joy, but I thank God that the reason I get up every Sunday morning and come here on fire is because there's some bread in Bethlehem. I'm not coming to church just to satisfy a social requirement. I'm coming to church because I need some bread. It's hell out there, it's hard out there, but I heard that there is a fountain and it's filled with blood, and it's drawn from Emmanuel's veins. We come to church because we need bread; we are hungry; we need sustenance from God. We need bread to make it from one day to the next. We need bread in order to handle that relationship, to raise children, to go to that hellhole of a job tomorrow.

"I was sinking deep in sin, far from the peaceful shore...but the Master heard my despairing cry and from the waters he lifted me." I did like Naomi and said bye-bye, Moab. Farewell, Moab. I've kept in touch with some folk in Bethlehem. I'm going back to the house of bread. I've found the bread house; I found Bethlehem.

A little bit of bread will carry you a long way. A little bit of bread will help you when you lose a loved one. A little bit of bread will help you when you lose your job. A little bit of bread will help you when you get a bad report from the doctor. A little bit of bread will help you when your house goes into foreclosure. A little bit of bread will help you if you don't have a house or health care insurance. A little bit of bread will help you out of your negative mindset. A little bit of bread will help you out of your abuse. A little bit of bread will give you a positive mindset. A little bit of bread will put running in your feet, clapping in your hands, joy bells in your heart, common sense in your mind, and love in your heart.

I thank Jesus that he didn't let me perish in Moab. And He didn't let Naomi perish there. Although she was bitter, she had some good things happen there in Moab. She had two beautiful daughters-in-law. Maintaining her sanity was a blessing. Lessons learned were a blessing. I'm glad she kept in touch with Bethlehem! There's bread of life, strength, expectation, and new beginnings in Bethlehem. She left her husband's mistakes and returned to Bethlehem, where she found bread and many blessings.

Don't stay in Moab. Return to the house of bread.

WHEN GOD DEALS
AN UNEVEN HAND

"Again, it will be like a man going on a journey, who called his servants and entrusted his property
to them. To one he gave five talents of money, to another two talents, and to another one talent,
each according to his ability. Then he went on his journey. The man who received the five talents
went at once and put his money to work and gained five more. So also, the one with the two talents
gained two more. But the man who had received the one talent went off, dug a hole in the ground
and hid his master's money. After a long time the master of those servants returned and settled
accounts with them. The man who had received the five talents brought the other five. 'Master,' he
said, 'you entrusted me with five talents. See, I have gained five more.' His master replied, 'Well
done, good and faithful servant! You have been faithful with a few things; I will put you in charge
of many things. Come and share your master's happiness!' The man with the two talents also came.
'Master,' he said, 'you entrusted me with two talents; see, I have gained two more.' His master
replied, 'Well done, good and faithful servant! You have been faithful with a few things; I will put
you in charge of many things. Come and share your master's happiness!' Then the man who had
received the one talent came. 'Master,' he said, 'I knew that you are a hard man, harvesting where
you have not sown and gathering where you have not scattered seed. So I was afraid and went
out and hid your talent in the ground. See, here is what belongs to you.' His master replied, 'You
wicked, lazy servant! So you knew that I harvest where I have not sown and gather where I have
not scattered seed? Well then, you should have put my money on deposit with the bankers, so that
when I returned I would have received it back with interest. Take the talent from him and give it
to the one who has the ten talents. For everyone who has will be given more, and he will have an
abundance. Whoever does not have, even what he has will be taken away from him. And throw

that worthless servant outside, into the darkness, where there will be weeping and gnashing of teeth." **Matthew 25:14-30, NIV**

I have become convinced in these brief but wonderful years that God has blessed me to live and to grow in His grace that genuine, authentic, and real faith can only be cultivated when we force ourselves to deal with the critical questions that nag at our human predicament. If I have anything against much of the preaching and much of the theology that is being propagated today—particularly in religious programming in radio, TV, and print—it is that so many are seeking to make the Christian journey appear to be an easy one: "Five Easy Steps to Learn How to Pray"; "Learn the Ten Proven Steps to Your Miracle." Anybody with a modicum of intelligence knows that the journey with Christ and the journey toward Christ is an uneven journey. And because it is uneven, there are things that happen along the way that could stymie us. There are many people who cannot handle the unevenness of their journey. Thus, many people become pessimistic, and some even leave the church altogether, primarily because they cannot make sense out of that which is nonsense.

Among the many attributes of God is the attribute that God is love. And beyond that, God is truth, God is beauty, God is holiness. But among the things that we never see anywhere in Scripture is the notion that God is fair. He never makes that claim. His Word does not have that in print. Yet so often when difficult things occur to us in life, the first response is "It isn't fair." And you are absolutely right. The problem comes, however, when we want to blame God for the unfairness.

When Thomas Jefferson sat down to write the Declaration of Independence, he began the preamble to that document with the words,

"We hold these truths to be self-evident, that all men are created equal, that they are endowed by their Creator with certain unalienable Rights, that among these are Life, Liberty and the pursuit of Happiness." But Mr. Jefferson was wrong. We are not created equal. In the creation of humankind, in one context, males and females share equality—but only in the sense of their gifts and abilities. There is an inequality when it comes to the male and the female. We are not equal when it comes to our biology, our anatomy, our physiology, and even when it comes to our emotional makeup. There are distinct differences among the two sexes. And in many instances one might tag those differences as being unfair. If all men and women were created equal, then that means that every baby ever born of a woman would come into the world with all five fingers on one hand, all five toes on one foot, and there would be no such thing as birth defects. We are not created equal.

In this parable that Jesus teaches about the kingdom of God, He tells of a wise master who, before taking a long journey, calls in his servants and begins to give them what the Word calls "talents." One might well redefine that and call these talents "opportunities." To one, he gave five; to a second, he gave two; and finally to the third, he gave one. Now, if one were going to employ the principle of fairness, fairness would suggest equality. Equality, therefore, means that in the dispensation of the talents or gifts or opportunities, all three should have received five, two, or one. Immediately, when there is this distinction (to one is given five, a second two, and finally to the third one), there is an inequality. This can be viewed as an uneven hand. And one cannot really fathom the depths of God's omniscience. Why is it that God places in some of us more gifts or more talents, and provides for some of us more opportunities than He does for others? I think today about how in some lives there are a myriad of gifts and how in other lives there is only one gift. But whether the gifts are many or one, the point is that there is a gift. There is nobody born without at least one gift, and many of us spend entirely too much time dealing with life's unfairness rather than dealing with its reality.

The idea for the dispensation of the talents, gifts, or opportunities was that something must be done with what is placed at each servant's disposal. When the master returns from his journey, he wants accountability. And there was a proud report from the one to whom he gave five: "I doubled mine. I now have ten." The master replied, "Well done, my good and faithful servant. You've been faithful over a few things. I'm going to make you ruler over many." In the second report, the man with two returned with four. And the same word of commendation was issued to him. But the third man was gripped by the principle of unfairness and allowed that grip to put him in such a devastating vice that he had the nerve to pointedly say to his master, "You are a hard man." He could not handle the fact that the others were given more talents than he possessed. And he said, "While the one with five may have come back with ten and the one with two has come back with four, the one that you gave me, I buried." And the Lord answers in the text—the mouth of the master comes down hard on the person with one, and he banishes that person to outer darkness because nothing at all was done with the one talent, the one gift, the one responsibility, the one resource placed at his disposal.

Now, here's the real life lesson that I want argue about today. We need to come down from this high horse of fairness, because if we are waiting for life to be fair to us, we will be waiting a long while because it will never happen. Too many of us are carrying baggage around from our childhood, because we feel somebody in our lives was unfair a long time ago. And if you're waiting for God to say something that He never intended to say, that, too, will never happen. Let it go! Not one jot or tittle of this Word will ever be changed: "I tell you the truth, until heaven and earth disappear, not the smallest letter, not the least stroke of a pen, will by any means disappear from the Law until everything is accomplished" (Matthew 5:18, NIV).

And even though life is unfair, and even though life is, as our mothers and fathers declare, "an uneven journey," we must first understand that in the unevenness of the journey we must first accept reality. We do not know why the fabric of life is woven with the stitch of unfairness. We cannot tap the omniscient mind of God and give to one another today a plausible and pliable explanation. I wish I could, but I cannot. But I've learned this much in my years of living: There are certain realities that we have to accept. We've got to accept that people are mean. We've got to accept that life will slap us on one side; and if we keep on living, it will slap us on the other side. We must accept the reality that all dreams will not come true, and that there are some dreams that will become a nightmare. Therefore, we must accept the reality that life, my brothers and sisters, is unfair.

Our faith, contrary to popular opinion, is a realistic faith. The faith of Jesus Christ does not paint an unrealistic picture of life for us. Everybody isn't given the same gifts nor will everybody get the same things out of life. But if we can proceed along the premise that life isn't fair, then we can brace ourselves for whatever thunder rolls, for whatever lightning flashes, and for whatever stormy winds may blow. Some of us live in the prison of an unrealistic mindset, always wanting for life to do for us what life has not done for anybody else. One day we will discover—I pray sooner than later—that in life we must learn to make our way through unfairness.

Has it ever dawned upon you that Jesus Christ—Son of the living God, Son of Mary, and Son of Joseph—was born in an unfair state? He was born a Jew, and a Jew in the ancient world is pretty much like being born a Black man in this country. He was born with an unfair disadvantage. The disadvantage was that He was born into a class of people who were maligned, who were enslaved, and who were entrapped. He was born in Bethlehem, raised in Nazareth, the son of a carpenter, and for the first 30 years of His life He plied His trade as a blue-collar worker. He lived the life of a peasant. He created enemies— Scribes, Pharisees, Herodians, and Sadducees. They all stood against Him. Those who were closest to Him, in the eventuality of things, turned on Him. Peter denied Him three times. Judas betrayed Him. All except one of His disciples abandoned Him. Yet, in the midst of all that unfairness, somehow He emerges with victory and triumph. With all of these disadvantages against Him, somehow He stands before us today as the greatest achiever in life; and He is the monumental example that as realistic and as unfair disadvantages are, God still possess the power and authority to makes a way out of no way.

Most of us have forgotten Betty Shabazz. She's been gone for a while now. What an unforgettable and towering symbol of strength she remains for us. She was female and Black—two strikes in a society that is sexist and racist—but in spite of it all, "she rose." She married one of the most radical figures in the latter part of the twentieth century, took on his convictions, gave birth to six beautiful Black girls, and at the age of 29 in the Audubon Ballroom in New York, she witnessed with the world her husband being cut down by an assassin—not by White faces but by Black faces. She raised those six daughters all by herself. She went on to get a Ph.D. and become a faculty member at Medgar Evers College. And you would think that by this time life would smooth out for her. As if all of that were not enough for Betty Shabazz, in 1997, her 12-year-old grandson—who is now 22 years old and in a mental institution today—set her body on fire, and she eventually died from third-degree burns.

How many of you have lived life long enough to discover that just when you think you have it all together, something else goes wrong. You stop and you say to yourself: "How much more do I have to take? How many more mountains do I have to climb? How many more tears do I have to shed? Why was I dealt such an uneven hand?"

Life isn't fair. Yet in the midst of it all, you must hang in there, in spite of the unfairness of your life. See, some of us have become so pessimistic, so negative because of the uneven hand that God has dealt us, that we live in a perpetual pity party—"P cubed." Too many of us are always complaining, comparing, competing, and always talking about what others are doing to stop us from prospering. Well, the ultimate question is not so much "What is being done to us?" but "What are we doing to ourselves?" Because if we accept the fact that life is unfair, there is very little that anyone can really do to us if we have focus, motivation, and a healthy self-perspective.

People who are pity partiers and who live in a "woe-is-me mindset" and who act like this third person in the parable tend to get upset with God because they don't have what somebody else has, and they are people who live in a state of inertia. Anybody who just wrangles eternally with how unfair life is, unfortunately, is wasting their time. "Inertia" means you're standing still, going nowhere fast. Somehow or other we have to learn to run anyhow. We still need to put our best foot forward and remain faithful to our calling. And we must believe that at the end of our journey we're going to hear, "Well done." And I also get the satisfaction of knowing that before I get to the end of the journey, in the midst of my struggle, God gives me power and strength to raise my head above my circumstances. No wonder the psalmist says, "My head will be exalted above the enemies who surround me" (Psalm 27:6). The Devil is a liar because in spite of our uneven hand, we're still going to be conquerors, because God has not birthed us to see us fail. Failures are really our lab for future victories. What serve as our obstacles and what may be our faltering moments are nothing more than hands on our backs that push us to our success.

See, most of us worship a God of comfort and a God of convenience. Most of us only know how to worship God with our praise through the good times. But that is not the only time we need to offer God our praise. We need to offer God our praise when things are not perfect in our lives. The God we serve is more than a God of comfort. He's more than a God of convenience. He is a God who is worthy of our praise even when we find ourselves between and betwixt some difficulty. He is a God who is at His best when His children are at their worst. When the journey becomes uneven and when the stumbling blocks mount beyond our abilities to carry them ourselves, God shifts into another gear. If one really wants to know who God is, one only needs to get into a tight spot. Get between an adversary and the deep blue sea and watch God change the situation around when we obey His word, seek His will, and follow His way.

Stop getting caught up in the five opportunities that somebody else has or the two gifts somebody else may possess. Thank God for what

He has entrusted you with. You may not have the fanciest house, but thank God you've got shelter over your head. You may not have a St. John suit on your flesh, but thank God you've got something to cover your body. You may not have a Gucci bag under one arm and a Coach purse under another, but thank God you've got a pocket to place two quarters in. We need to thank God for what we do have and stop having our pity parties. Again, pity parties create people who live in inertia, and people who are in inertia don't really get anywhere.

Jeremiah A. Wright, Jr. preached a sermon some years ago entitled "Black Man, What Makes You So Strong?" He said it isn't the house where we live. It's not the education we have. It's not the job we go to every day. It's not the material and intangible possessions that we possess. But what makes us so strong, as a people, is our tenacity and our faith that declare if God is for us, that's bigger and better than all of the world against us.

During graduation time of the year, I always surf C-SPAN. I want to hear the commencement speeches that are being given on our college campuses and universities. I've been discouraged and disheartened because we no longer invite to college campuses people who will talk about God. Many commencement speakers want to talk about what has been the faith of their academic pilgrimage and how they have achieved their degrees, but nobody appears to talk about God. Who do we invite? We invite celebrities, and we invite money mongrels. We want people to give commencement addresses who are going to donate money to our colleges and our universities. And while they have a story to tell, we need to put somebody on the stage who has been through hell and lived to talk about it—somebody Black who can stand up on a stage and say, "For 388 years, the deck has been stacked against us. But here we are." And somebody ought to have the courage to stand up and say that behind it all was a God who knows how to shuffle the cards.

When was the last time you heard talk about God at a high school commencement or a college exercise? You'll hear it on a seminary campus because that's where we talk about God. But on these nominal college and university campuses, nobody talks about God. It's hard even getting an "amen."

I came to church through the rain this morning, just like many of you. All of us could have had an accident. I saw a big old truck turned over on its side, but through the rain, we made it here safely. I saw a parallel. How many of us know what it is to come through the rain, and looking on the side of your road we see many a life that's been overturned? But there is a God who walks with us. And there's a God who talks with us, especially when life deals us an uneven hand.

To live in a state of complaint, to reside in a ditch of inertia, is not to allow God to change our hands. Now we need to remember our card-playing days. In any card game, like pinochle or 500 gin rummy, we keep acquiring cards and we keep getting rid of cards because at any moment in the game, depending upon the cards received, our hand can change. And see, the problem with chronic complainers and people who consistently display temper tantrums is that they keep holding the same cards and don't realize that God's got some more cards in the deck. We don't know when the heart, club, diamond, or spade is going to come up. But if we keep plucking from the deck—and if we hang in there a little while longer, God's got to give us a new card that will change our losing hand to a winning hand.

Have you had your hand change recently? Have you felt like giving up? Have you felt like throwing in your hand? I don't know your unique situation, but I trust God would say to everyone, "Hang in there a little while longer, and keep plucking from the deck of life." Pluck from your praise. Pluck from your worship. Pluck from your Bible study. Pluck from your ministry. Pluck from your Sunday school class. And if you keep on plucking, you are going to get a card that's going to change your hand. Please know that if you hang in there long enough, God will change your hand.

In 1839, some slaves were being brought to this country. A group of them on a vessel called the Amistad hijacked the slave ship and took it over. They took over the Amistad somewhere around Cuba. They didn't know where they were going. They didn't know anything about ships. But somehow or another, those navigationally challenged Black slaves from West Africa commandeered a ship. Somehow they managed to steer the boat without any them having had any knowledge of ship steering. They were agrarian people. They were agriculturalists. They ended up somewhere off the coast of Long Island in New York. Now, geographically, Cuba is down beyond the tip of Florida. That means they came up the East Coast through the watery deep of the Atlantic. How did those Black folk get all the way from Cuba to Long Island, New York, when not one of them had any navigating intelligence? The ship never turned over. The ship never angled to go down to South America. It did not angle to go farther east out into the Atlantic. And when they got up into the Long Island area, that's where they were captured and enslaved. Now you can imagine; they thought they were going back to Africa, but they were coming to America to experience our brand of apartheid.

When I first read the story of the Amistad many, many years ago, I thought to myself, how disheartening that must have been—to overtake the ship, commandeer it, believe you're on your way back home, and then end up in an oppressive government that wanted to enslave you in the beginning. They were put into slave chains. But remember, God always provides us with another card. John Quincy Adams, no longer the president, but back in law practice, decided to defend these fifty-three West African slaves. And guess what? Those slaves, not knowing anything about English, with people like Samuel Baldwin, Lewis Tappan, and Theodore Joadson, all decent White men who had in their minds the notion of the freedom of the African American, got together and put their sums of money together and fought with John Quincy Adams until the fifty-three Amistad-commandeering slaves became free. And they were put on a ship and sent back to Africa. They were never totally enslaved here. God somehow changed their hand.

I don't care how many times you've plucked the wrong card; keep on plucking, and one of these days your hand is going to change. But until it transforms, be like Job and say, "I will wait for my change to come" (Job 14:14). We all know that He may not come when we want Him, but when He shows up, He's always right on time. We've got to accept our hand that has been dealt to us but not be resigned to it. We must not waste our time getting caught up in what we don't have, because in doing that, in the eventuality of reality we will end up in a state of inertia. We must stick with our faith, believing somehow that at any moment God will change our hand. But until the change comes, we must deal with the hand we have rather than complain about the hand we have.

We must thank God that we have a hand. It may not be the hand we want, but at least it's a hand we can play. It doesn't matter whether you have five, two, or one gift(s), and/or talent(s); the blessing is you don't have zero. And if we just have one, we ought to play our one card because our one card just may be our trump card. And if we just have one trump card, we can hang in there until our hand changes. And that's why Job said, "I'm going to wait until my change comes because after He's tried me, I shall come forth as pure gold" (Job 14:14; 23:10).

That's the genius of Black people. We have been able to shout even when we thought we didn't have anything to shout about. But we do have something to shout about because God gave us a hand with the Ultimate Trump Card. He gave us Jesus the Christ! And we ought to praise Him today, because regardless of our current hand, regardless of our current situation, regardless of our current tribulation, we can always play our Ultimate Trump Card, Jesus the Christ. It does not matter what we face, Jesus trumps it. It does not matter who is against us, Jesus trumps them. The fact is that in our hand Jesus has placed another card, the card of faith in His power to balance our uneven hand of life.

The last thing you want to do in a card game is throw in your hand. Well, if you are unwilling to throw in your hand at the pinochle table, why throw in your hand at the table of life? Real card players hold their cards close to the chest. And every now and then, you have to do this: just check out the card and make sure it's the same card. Then once you check out the card, you can look at the game and say, "Yeah, I'm still smiling, because I've got the God Card." We can learn to play our God Card, where victory is always assured. Ultimately, it is about His will and not ours.

I remember when I was a little boy and children used to laugh at me because of my eye. I didn't have the custom prosthesis that I wear today. If you had seen me when I was a little boy and all through college, you'd have seen what they call a stock prosthesis—a false eye. And I remember being laughed at one day, and I came home crying. I was a little bitty fellow. And I buried my head in my mother's apron and she said, "What's wrong, Son?" I said, "Mama, they keep laughing at me because of my eye." And she took my little face, lifted it out of her apron, held my face in her hand, and she said, "You are my beautiful Black Son." And I remember saying to Mama, "Mama, how come God didn't give me two eyes like everybody else?" She said, "I'm going to tell you something." Holding my face in her hands, she said, "I don't know why." But she said, "You don't need two eyes to do God's will. Use the one you got and leave the rest to God." And so I say today, use what you have and leave the rest to God—because what God has for you is for *you*.

God's ways are not our ways, and God's thoughts are not our thoughts. As high as the heavens are above the earth, so high are God's ways above our ways and God's thoughts above our thoughts (Isaiah 55:8-9). I've got to accept the reality but not be resigned to the reality. And in the acceptance of the reality, I must not live in a state of inertia and waste my time brooding and complaining because life is unfair.

Now, take a deep breath and give God praise and celebrate the hand you have! Stop complaining about what you don't have, and thank Him for the hand you do have. Whatever you have, thank the Lord for it and watch God multiply it. Remain faithful to God and God will remain faithful to you. Always remember the hand that God deals us is the hand that He knows we can play. Remain faithful to your hand and to the God who dealt you the hand. Remember that you have the God Card.

STANDING ON SHAKY GROUND

It happened in the spring of the year, at the time when kings go out to battle, that David sent Joab and his servants with him, and all Israel; and they destroyed the people of Ammon and besieged Rabbah. But David remained at Jerusalem. Then it happened one evening that David arose from his bed and walked on the roof of the king's house. And from the roof he saw a woman bathing, and the woman was very beautiful to behold. So David sent and inquired about the woman. And someone said, "Is this not Bathsheba, the daughter of Eliam, the wife of Uriah the Hittite?" Then David sent messengers, and took her; and she came to him, and he lay with her, for she was cleansed from her impurity; and she returned to her house. **2 Samuel 11:1-4, NKJV**

Do you know what it is like to be on shaky ground? Mark Madoff, Bernard Madoff's son, was on shaky ground. Here was a man who obviously had been wrestling with deep inner conflicts. His father, in jail for 150 years for propagating and promoting one of the greatest economic scandals ever to hit this country, swindled people out of billions of dollars. The suicide death of Mark Madoff is the tragedy of someone who lived on shaky ground. He was not guilty of his father's sins, but there were those who contend that he must have been guilty and he must have known something because he was very much involved in his father's financial empire. No wrongdoing was ever presented against Mark. Nothing of a corrupt nature about Mark was ever revealed. However, little things were being said. We are told that there were powers that be who wanted to bring Mark to court, to prosecute him because they believed that he was a part of the whole Ponzi scheme. Here was a young man very much economically stable in his own right, but he could not handle the whispers and innuendoes that people were saying about him. He was on shaky emotional, spiritual, and psychological ground.

That story and our text show us what can happen when we are not leaning on the solid rock, when we are on shaky ground. At the time of our text it is springtime in Israel. The winter or rainy season has passed. It was the time for kings and all of the other ancient peoples of the world at that point in history to lead their troops into battle. They didn't fight in the wintertime because the wintertime was not so much cold as it was wet. The roads were muddy. Late spring was the ideal time for fighting.

At this point in Israel's history, the enemy is not the Philistines, but the enemy is represented by the Ammonites. There's been a battle and now the Ammonites are walled up in protective security behind the walls of a place called Rabbah. This was the time for David, the king and commander-in-chief, to lead his men in battle against the Ammonites. However, David elects to abdicate his responsibility and remain at home to enjoy the luxury of his domicile. Instead of leading his men into battle, David designates Joab, his chief lieutenant and alter-ego, to lead the army. When it's time to fight again, David, for whatever reasons, decides that he's going to sit this war out. And that's sign number one that he was on shaky ground.

Idle time is always the devil's workshop. I don't care how young or how old you are, you need to be doing something. The last thing you need to do is sit home on your rusty dusty doing absolutely nothing. God does not give you life simply to sit around. You ought to be giving

God some kind of creative time. God has not given you life to sit back and look at what you have done.

David is not only king; David is commander-in-chief, and it's time to fight, but David decides to stay at home when he should be in battle. When David is not at his place of responsibility, when he's not at his position of task, that's when the devil allows him to choose and make a decision that does not only impact him, but it also wreaks havoc in his family. It is at this juncture that David stands on shaky ground because what occurs in place of his not going into battle creates consequences he will suffer for the rest of his life. It is now that his eyes fall upon the beautiful Bathsheba, and we know the rest of the story.

How do you know when you are standing on shaky ground? We are standing on shaky ground when we are not in position, when we are not at our places of task and responsibility. We're on shaky ground when we abdicate responsibility for whatever reason, when we relinquish responsibility. God has assigned everyone a certain responsibility, and God anoints everyone to take a certain responsibility. David was commander-in-chief. He's the king. He is to go out and fight with his men. Even if David had gone to the battlefield and not actively engaged in fighting, his presence would have done much to encourage his men and push them to victory.

Every now and then, I need to know that my leader is with me. I need to know that the Lord is with me. I know He is Spirit, but the scripture says that He sits at the right hand of the Father. And if the Bible is correct, the book says that when Stephen was stoned, when Stephen got in trouble, Jesus stood up. I need to know every now and then that the Lord is standing up when all hell breaks loose around me.

How many of you know that when you get in trouble, the Lord doesn't sit down, but the Lord will stand up in your circumstance? Sometimes you just need to see the leader. Even though he may not fight, you need to know that the leader is on the battlefield.

Nobody is in the kingdom of God without an assignment, and God does not give an assignment without anointing. We must never forget that when we are out of position and not at our place of task and responsibility we are in danger of losing our anointing. We are anointed for certain tasks and responsibilities. When we are not doing what God has anointed and appointed us to do then we become spiritually weak, anemic, and impotent. We may well have God's presence, but not His anointing. You will always have God's presence because He promised never to leave you nor forsake you, but just because you have His presence does not mean you have His anointing.

If you want to know why some people fail miserably in the church, it is because they are not in their proper position. Because when you are anointed to do something, God empowers you. You don't have to tell anybody you have the anointing. When the anointing is on you, it will show. I've listened to a whole lot of people preach, but they don't have any power. I've listened to a whole lot of folks sing, but they don't have any power. I've listened to a whole lot of people play an organ, but they don't have any power. When you are at the place where you are born to be, doing what God told you to do, God will anoint you. He will anoint you for your assignment.

Some of you want to know why you're spiritually weak, why you are religiously anemic, why you are biblically inept? It is because you are not where God wants you to be. God doesn't want you to simply occupy a pew on Sunday one week out of every month. God wants you at a place of responsibility. Are you ready for this? Again, you will always have God's presence because He promised never to leave you nor forsake you, but just because you have His presence does not mean you have His anointing.

David had the anointing when tending his father's sheep; thus, he subdued the lion and the bear. He was at his place of responsibility. He was able to defeat Goliath even though he was a boy because he was at his place of responsibility. However, now David is on shaky ground because he is not where his anointing mandates him to be. He is at home when he should be on the battlefield.

The second lesson David teaches us is that we are standing on shaky ground when we relax on our laurels. Not only does David vacate his place of task, but he also relaxes on his laurels. This is the reason David is out of position. He feels no need to fight because his goals have been reached, his objectives have been fulfilled, and he was experiencing fulfillment and satisfaction. Here's a man who was relaxing on his laurels.

Look at the litany of David's accomplishments: Israel was united in a solidified monarchy. Southern Judah and Northern Israel were one with Jerusalem as the capital. Israel's borders have been expanded. The country was prospering. David was now firmly established in the minds and hearts of the people. David has subdued the Edomites, the Moabites, the Amalekites, the Ammonites, and the Philistines. In the modern colloquial expression, David had it "going on!"

For 33 years, David would now rule in Jerusalem. The boundaries were expanded. Prosperity had come to the kingdom. David was now the unchallenged ruler in the minds and the hearts of Israel. Saul was dead so he was no longer David's antagonist. So David says, "Alright, all things are in order. All of my ducks are in a row. I can sit back and enjoy life. I deserve a break today."

But David's decision to relax was not wise at all. It was not really the time to relax. He had an uncompleted task. Although David had met the challenge of the Ammonite rebellion following Nahash's death (2 Samuel 10:6-14), he had not eliminated the Ammonite threat. In the previous fight with Israel the Ammonites has merely retreated behind the protective walls of Rabbah and remained virtually unscathed. The proximity of the Ammonites to the tribal territories of Gad and Manasseh meant that David could not ignore this menacing neighbor. David needed to lead this battle in order to erase the Ammonites' threat and protect the territories of Gath and Mahanaim. This was not a time to relax. David had won the battle, but not the war. One of the reasons some of us remain spiritually weak and anemic is because we win the battle, but we forget that the war still goes on. Each minor victory is designed to help you win the major war.

You ought to be careful the older you get about what you do and don't do, how you think and don't think. When you relax on your laurels, you can get in trouble. I don't care how young or how old, not one of us can ever afford to relax on our laurels. We must remain vigilant because "the devil is like a roaring lion seeking to devour whom he may!" In the words of Robert Frost, we have "miles to go before we sleep!" All of us have unfinished and uncompleted tasks!

Jesus learned this in Gethsemane when three times He asked for the cup's removal and the Father said "No!" God said, "Your assignment is more than preaching. Your assignment is more than teaching. I did not send you into the world only to be a miracle worker. I sent you to go up on a hill called Calvary. I sent you to die between the living and the dead. You've got an unfinished task."

Is anybody glad that Jesus went up on a hill called Calvary? Is anybody glad that they put nails in his hands? Is anybody glad that they put a sword in his side? Somebody ought to be able to shout, "There is a fountain and it's filled with blood drawn from Immanuel's veins where sinners plunge." Are you glad that you're covered by the blood?

Finally, David teaches us that we are on shaky ground when we abuse power and authority for personal advantage. When you get position, when you get power, when you get authority, you can't start smelling yourself. That's an old southern colloquial expression; you start smelling yourself. Can I put it another way? You get bigger than your britches and every now and then when you start smelling yourself, God's got to knock you down to size. David abused his power.

David sits out the war at springtime—he is not at his place of responsibility, and he is relaxing on his laurels, knowing that he ought to be out there fighting the Ammonites. In his idle time, he walks out on his balcony and his eye falls upon Bathsheba, who is well within her right to bathe upon her balcony. It's believed that she may have been taking a ritual bath marking the end of her menstrual cycle. David's house was located on the highest ground within the old Jebusite fortress where David lived, and from his rooftop he has a commanding view of the city. Bathsheba's roof could have had an enclosed courtyard prohibiting normal view, but from David's perched position he has a commanding view of an enclosed space not available to one at ground level. If he had been on ground level, she would have been obscured from human view, but because he's elevated—he's elevated in position, he's elevated in authority, he's elevated in power, and he's elevated in geography—he sees her.

David asks the messenger about Bathsheeba, "Who is this woman?" The messenger looks back at David and says, "That's Eliam's daughter, one of your most loyal fighters. It's Uriah's wife and Ahithophel's granddaughter. Ahithophel is one of your noble counselors. Come on, king, you know who she is." Now this messenger cannot be too blunt because, after all, David is the king, so the messenger has to stay within certain respectable boundaries. He fetches the woman and the woman comes. Somebody might say, "Well, why did she go?" Because when the king calls, it was not optional; it was a mandate. Nothing, in all of my years of preaching, nothing in my research, has ever indicated that Bathsheba did anything wrong. There is no evidence that Bathsheba was a temptress. There is no hint that she was flirtatious, fickle, or foolish. She never tried to charm him. I believe that David was the culprit. If David were in a court of law today, the minimum charge might be sexual harassment. The maximum charge might have been rape. Nobody will convince me that he hadn't had his eye on her a long time. Now that Uriah is off on the battlefield somewhere near Rabbah fighting the Ammonites with Joab, David saw his moment, and the text says that she comes to him after her cycle, when her purification had ended.

When the devil gets on you, you forget all about logic. Reason takes flight. The text says that David lies with her knowing he used his position, power, and authority for personal advantage. This is something people ought never do, especially in the church! Power, position, and authority are for God's glory and not self-aggrandizement.

Don't just leave it on the sexual plane. We can abuse power in many different ways and places—in politics, in war, in society, in families. We abuse our parental authority by demanding our children to become what we want them to become rather than letting them carve out their own destiny. Our children can manipulate us and get us to do stuff that we know doesn't help them grow into knowledgeable people. Abuse takes place on all levels, and power corrupts. That's why you and I must be eternally vigilant.

We celebrate Christmas because God had to send somebody to get you and me straight. We were getting ready to mess up our eternal salvation. That's why somebody ought to thank God that Jesus came through forty and two generations. The good news is that the Lord can save you from anything. The Lord can save you from anybody. The Lord will rescue you from your own devilish acts. Does anybody have a testimony that had it not been for the Lord on my side, somebody tell me where would I be? I'm glad that I serve a God who can make me know when I'm wrong. I acknowledge my transgression and my sins are ever before me. I know I've been on shaky ground.

I remember many years ago when I was in Chicago preaching a revival and a certain preacher in that town had been caught in an indiscretion. There were ladies standing in line getting ready to speak to me. They were dogging the preacher and talking about what a shame it was and how they were not going to ever listen to him preach again.

When they got up to me, I said, "I couldn't help but overhear how you were talking about Dr. So-and-So and how you'll never listen to him preach again because of his indiscretion." I asked what their favorite passage of Scripture was and one lady said the 23rd Psalm, the Lord is my shepherd. I asked the other lady and she said the 27th Psalm, the Lord is my light and my salvation. I asked, "Do you still read them?" They said yes. I said, "Do they still make you happy?" They said yes. I said, "Do you know who wrote those Psalms? Do you know when he had written them? He didn't write them before Bathsheba. He wrote them after Bathsheba, so if you're not going to listen to the preacher, shut up your Bible and don't read the 23rd Psalm anymore. Shut up your Bible and don't read the 27th Psalm anymore." If the Lord could forgive David, I know that the Lord will forgive the preacher who was caught in an indiscretion. I love calling on David.

> Blessed is the man Who walks not in the counsel of the ungodly, Nor stands in the path of sinners, Nor sits in the seat of the scornful; But his delight is in the law of the LORD, And in His law he meditates day and night. He shall be like a tree Planted by the rivers of water, That brings forth its fruit in its season, Whose leaf also shall not wither; And whatever he does shall prosper. The ungodly are not so, But are like the chaff which the wind drives away. Therefore the ungodly shall not stand in the judgment, Nor sinners in the congregation of the righteous. For the LORD knows the way of the righteous, But the way of the ungodly shall perish. (Psalm 1, NKJV)

Can I talk about David? "I will bless the LORD at all times; His praise shall continually be in my mouth" (Psalm 34:1, NKJV). Can I talk about David? "LORD, you have searched me and known me. You know my sitting down and my rising up" (Psalm 139:1-2a, NKJV). Can I talk about David? "Who may ascend into the hill of the LORD? Or who may stand in His holy place? He who has clean hands and a pure heart, Who has not lifted up his soul to an idol, Nor sworn deceitfully. He shall receive blessing from the LORD, And righteousness from the God of his salvation" (Psalm 24:3-5, NKJV). Can I talk about David? "Yea, though I walk through the valley of the shadow of death, I will fear no evil; For You are with me; Your rod and Your staff, they comfort me. You prepare a table before me in the presence of my enemies; You anoint my head with oil; My cup runs over. Surely goodness and mercy shall follow me All the days of my life; And I will dwell in the house of the LORD Forever" (Psalm 23:4-6, NKJV).

"Lift up your heads, O you gates! And be lifted up, you everlasting doors! And the King of glory shall come in. Who is this King of glory? The LORD strong and mighty, The LORD mighty in battle" (Psalm 24:7-8, NKJV). You ought to start looking up instead of looking down, because I will lift up mine eyes unto the heels from which cometh my help—all of my help cometh from the LORD.

Is anybody on shaky ground? You've got to make a decision that's going to impact the rest of your life. Is anybody on shaky ground? This isn't the time to hide it. There's only one way out: "I acknowledge my transgressions . . ." (Psalm 51:3, NKJV).

Come to the altar of God. Use David's story as a lesson, as a warning, as a reminder of God's faithfulness and God's forgiveness. Get off shaky ground. Get in your rightful position. Do it for God!

DON'T MISS
HIS PRESENCE

Now Jacob went out from Beersheba and went toward Haran. So he came to a certain place and stayed there all night, because the sun had set. And he took one of the stones of that place and put it at his head, and he lay down in that place to sleep. Then he dreamed, and behold, a ladder was set up on the earth, and its top reached to heaven; and there the angels of God were ascending and descending on it. And behold, the LORD stood above it and said: "I am the LORD God of Abraham your father and the God of Isaac; the land on which you lie I will give to you and your descendants. Also your descendants shall be as the dust of the earth; you shall spread abroad to the west and the east, to the north and the south; and in you and in your seed all the families of the earth shall be blessed. Behold, I am with you and will keep you wherever you go, and will bring you back to this land; for I will not leave you until I have done what I have spoken to you." Then Jacob awoke from his sleep and said, "Surely the LORD is in this place, and I did not know it." And he was afraid and said, "How awesome is this place! This is none other than the house of God, and this is the gate of heaven!" **Genesis 28:10-17, NKJV**

I think that I speak for every sincere and authentic Christian when I say that we live to enjoy the presence of God. Anyone with a modicum of spiritual intelligence clamors for the presence of the living God. David, the psalmist, said it best in Psalm 16:11: "In thy presence is fullness of joy."

You will not disagree with me when I say that we live in a world of cacophony and dissonance. There is so much negativity, pessimism, sickness, disease, violence, political misdeeds, and sexual, emotional, and mental abuse. We need the presence of the Lord, for in His presence is not only joy, but also "a peace that passes all human understanding."

How unfortunate that there are persons who live on a daily basis and never sense the presence of God. They are overwhelmed by internal strife within as well as situations and circumstances without. The presence of God can be known anywhere because God is omnipresent. Again the psalmist comes to our aid: "Where can I go from Your Spirit? Or where can I flee from Your presence? If I ascend into heaven, You are there; If I make my bed in hell, behold, You are there. If I take the wings of the morning, And dwell in the uttermost parts of the sea, Even there Your hand shall lead me, And your right hand shall hold me" (Psalm 139:7-10, NKJV).

Never forget that because of God's omnipresence, He is always available. The task is for you and me to avail ourselves to His presence that we might be lifted, encouraged, and inspired by Him. I believe that the presence of God gives tremendous weight, gravitas, strength, and encouragement to all who sincerely believe in Him and call upon His name. I'm further convinced that there are those of us who perhaps are lacking when it comes to really sensing the presence of God, primarily because we are weak when it comes to our prayer and devotional living. The presence of God on a daily basis must be cultivated. A farmer does not simply sit in his house and wait for the harvest to come. The farmer painstakingly plants his seed, works the ground, fertilizes it, awaits the rain and the sun that can only come from God, and in a certain amount of time, a harvest does come.

The greater tragedy is that there are people who worship in the sanctuary week after week, Sunday after Sunday, and sometimes leave having never experienced the presence of God. We are to "enter his gates with thanksgiving and come into his courts with praise." Some never do this because they are unable to put aside the secular when they enter the sacred place. These are well-meaning and well-intentioned people. However, the music, the reading of the scriptures, the prayers, the fellowship of the saints, and even the preaching of the Gospel, for whatever reason, does not usher in the presence of God. These people are spectators and not participants. They are always on the outside looking in!

Now in our text, we see someone who finds the beauty and peace of being in God's presence because he has known life without God's presence. Our text is talking about Jacob. And all of us know of Abraham, we know of Isaac, and now we come to Jacob. One of the reasons I love preaching about Jacob is because of what I call Jacob's rascality. And the reason that I love to talk about his rascality is because there is rascality in all of us. You've got some rascal in you, and I've got some rascal in me, and God seeks always to harness that rascality in us, so that He can diminish it to the point that we become His servants, and that He molds that rascality, takes it, and uses it even to His glory.

Prior to the story in the today's text, Jacob had schemed with his mother to get the blessing from Isaac that rightfully belonged to Esau— and that's a bad thing when you have a rascal for a mother. It's one thing for you to be a rascal, but if your mama's a rascal, that's really a difficult thing. Mother and son, in their rascality, have finagled the blessing from Isaac, who is half blind, and now Esau realizes that the blessing that rightfully belonged to him had been given to Jacob. And Jacob, to save his life, must get out of town.

The rascality of Jacob's mother has covered all the bases. She has already planned Jacob's escape. Provision has already been made 400 miles away in Haran, particularly in Paddan-aram, for Jacob to live with his uncle, Rebecca's brother, Laban. And so Jacob gets out of town quickly. With haste, he leaves the only familiar surrounding that he knows. 400 miles is a long way to travel on foot. He doesn't even have a donkey.

The scriptures tell us that Jacob must go to Haran to secure a wife outside of Canaan. However, the real reason for Jacob's departure is that his brother has vowed to kill him for his deceit and trickery. It is while Jacob makes his way to Haran, specifically Paddan-aram, that fatigue overtakes him. He has traveled 70 miles, and he gets tired. The text says that the sun has set. Dusk is about to become darkness, and this rascal of a human being places his head upon a rock. The rock becomes his pillow, and the canopy of the night stars becomes his blanket. He is at Luz (or what he will rename as Bethel). He camps for the night and dreams that God has stretched a ladder from the height of the eternities down to the earth, and upon that ladder are those stellar creatures—angels—ascending and descending. But it is God himself who speaks at the top of the ladder to remind Jacob of the promise: "I am the God of your grandfather, I am the God of your daddy, and I am still the God of you, despite your rascal behavior."

Now, it's a wonderful thing to know that God sticks with us in our rascal moments, even when those close to us abandon us. Was it not David who said that "even when my mother and father forsake me, then the LORD will take me up"? It's a wonderful thing to feel the presence of God when everybody else has abandoned you. And there are times when we feel utterly abandoned. It may not necessarily be so, but given what is the time, the temper, and the tenor of our experience, we can feel all by ourselves. And yet, in the nocturne, God visits this man in a dream, and he awakens from the dream and declares these words: "Surely the LORD is in this place and I knew it not!" Why couldn't Jacob initially recognize that mountain place where he camped as the place of the presence of God?

Jacob's difficulty was that this place was barren. There was no botanical beauty about Luz. There were no flowers, no lush green grass, no trees standing in erect majesty. There was nothing lovely about Luz. The name sounds bad—Luz. There was no excitement in Luz, no enthusiasm in Luz. The landscape was barren with nothing but rocks and dust. So often we forget that God supersedes what is pleasing to the eye. We have a tendency, on occasion, to limit God to building beauty or ornateness. We sometimes fail to realize God's omnipresence and God's beauty. The beauty of God is not so much in a place as it is *in Him*. Even though the place may be barren and not physically appealing to the eye, God remains present and beautiful for He is "the fairest of ten thousand!"

One must look for God in unsuspecting places: David sensed the presence of God when he walked through the valley of the shadow of death but felt no evil; Daniel sensed the presence of God in that lions' den; the Hebrew boys sensed the presence of God in the fiery furnace; the shepherds sensed the presence of God in the open fields of Bethlehem; Paul and Silas sensed the presence of God in that Philippian jail cell; John sensed the presence of God on the Isle of Patmos; Dr. Martin Luther King, Jr. sensed the presence of God in that prison in Birmingham, Alabama.

Jacob was not only in a barren place, physically, but he was in a barren place emotionally, spiritually, and psychologically because this was his first time away from home. He was not the outdoorsman his brother was. Jacob was a "mama's boy" who enjoyed the pampering of his mother. One can only imagine how frightened, scared, and fearful Jacob was. This was his first night away from home and he spends it under the stars with a stone for his pillow and the canopy of the heavens for his blanket.

We must never forget that God is with us in the barren places and moments of our lives. We are never alone. Every now and then, life will rock you from side to side, and the dust will so cloud the vision of Christ that it's hard to be in His presence. But the good news is God is there—God is in barren places. He promised to "never leave us alone"! He promised to be with us always, "even until the end of the world"! But barrenness can make you miss God's presence.

Jacob also missed the presence of God because he went to sleep preoccupied with his scandalous behavior. He's not just dealing with physical barrenness. He's got some emotional and psychological barrenness. He had deceived his father by making him think he was Esau. He had taken the blessing that legitimately belonged to Esau as the firstborn. (Do not forget that earlier Jacob made Esau give him the birthright in exchange for a bowl of soup. Esau thought more of his stomach than his birthright.) It is to Jacob's credit that he has a conscience. The problem comes with that individual who says and does destructive things with no awareness of wrongdoing at all. Your conscience can interfere with your rest and the presence of God! So Jacob went to sleep with his conscience not just bothering him, but battering him.

We should be able to relate to Jacob's restless night. Something's wrong with anybody who claims Jesus Christ, knowingly does wrong, and can sleep all night long. Anybody who can talk about somebody like a dog, and know you're wrong, and sleep all night, has no God in him or her. Your conscience ought to make you so shiver in your shoes that you're not able to sleep because you know that there is something wrong. You are not the victim; you are the perpetrator.

One of the hardest things in life is getting people to understand that they are not always the victim. Many of us occupy perpetrator status. In a way, you feel sorry for Jacob, but in a way, you don't, because he has brought his predicament on himself. His rascality, his scandalous behavior bothers him. It goes all the way back to the way that he got the birthright, the way he tricked his brother and father.

There is always the problem of allowing life to be visualized on the level of the horizontal, like Jacob did. We can become so saturated with the horizontal realities of life that our vertical relationship with God becomes impaired. We drag our problems to bed and into the church pew for worship. We become inundated with our horizontal difficulties—relational, economic, health, social, and employment issues. The ladder in the text with angels ascending and descending represents our vertical relationship with God. If all one does is concentrate on the horizontal, one will end up depressed, angry, and frustrated. However, when one turns from the horizontal to the vertical one's mindset and focus change: "I will life up mine eyes unto the hills from whence cometh my help! My help cometh from the LORD." "Lift up your heads, o ye gates, and even lift them up ye everlasting doors and the King of glory will come in." "Father, I stretch my hand to thee, no other help I know!" The horizontal is depressing, but the vertical is uplifting! The horizontal is frustrating, but the vertical is hopeful! The horizontal is negative, but the vertical is positive!

Finally, Jacob missed the presence of God because he feared his brother's vengeance and retaliation. Do not forget that Esau vowed to kill his brother because of his deception and trickery. It must be a terrible thing to live life having to always look over your shoulder. Jacob left home and had to sleep with the fear that at any moment Esau might appear and slay him as Cain had slain Abel. Cain may be dead, but "Cainism" is still alive. It's hard to sleep and feel the presence of God when you know that you are responsible for the ruptured relationship; that you are not the victim, but the perpetrator; and that at any hour of the day or night vengeance and retaliation might come.

That's a terrible way to live. It's a horrible way to live. How many of us are living life crippled by some unresolved something in our yesterday? You and I know people who can never live positive, fulfilling lives because they are crippled by yesterday. A whole lot of folk have not learned how to forgive themselves. I spoke to an elderly man not too long ago who said to me when I had finished preaching, "I need a word with you. I believe you can help me with my circumstance." He said, "I did something 30 years ago that I've not gotten over. I've asked God to forgive me, and I asked the person to whom I had done the wrong to forgive me, and they both have forgiven me. But I live perpetually in my own guilt." That's a hell that I would not wish upon anyone.

God's grace and mercy can plumb the depths of any circumstance. And you must learn to be able to rise out of the ditch of your own pain, knowing that God can forgive you of anything—anything. The only thing that the Scripture says God will not forgive us for is blasphemy against the Holy Ghost. Some of you are so holy that you always hold things against people. And a whole lot of people are crippled by their own guilt, and live in a ditch of frustration because there are always people who won't let them forget what they used to do, who they used to do it with.

This is why God let Jacob fall asleep and dream. The ladder with the ascending and descending angels is quite inspiring. But what is most inspiring is the promise God makes to Jacob to bless him and his offspring and bring him back to the land of his fathers. In other words, if one has the promise of God, one can feel the presence of God! When both the promise and the presence of God come together, all fears become vanquished. Despite Jacob's rascality, despite his scandalous behavior, how he got the birthright and the blessing from Esau, notice what God does *not* say in the dream. He says, "I am the God of your grandfather, Abraham. I am the God of your father, Isaac. I am your God." He says, "I will bless you, and I will bring you again into the land that you are lying on. Your seed shall be greater than the dust of the earth." But he never mentioned Jacob's rascality! He never said a word about his scandalous behavior. That's radically different from how we act. On the night when God meets Jacob in the dream, when you would think he would bring up the mess, when you think he would register the rascality, he says absolutely nothing about it.

Shall I blow your mind even more? It's not recorded anywhere that Jacob even asks for mercy. He never asks for grace. He never asks for forgiveness. But God gave it to him anyhow. Even when I was out there, young, dumb, and stupid, and doing stuff that was crazy, God gave me grace anyhow. When I should have died out there, God gave me mercy. When I never asked for forgiveness, God gave it to me. That's why I praise him. That's why I shout. That's why I give him glory because he didn't have to do it. I said he did not have to do it, but he did. His thoughts are not our thoughts! God gives me what I need, even when I don't ask for it. Hallelujah!

No wonder Jacob renames Luz, Bethel! Bethel represents the presence—the house or gateway to heaven!

A WONDERFUL TIME
IN THE STORM!

On the same day, when evening had come, He said to them, "Let us cross over to the other side." Now when they had left the multitude, they took Him along in the boat as He was. And other little boats were also with Him. And a great windstorm arose, and the waves beat into the boat, so that it was already filling. But He was in the stern, asleep on a pillow. And they awoke Him and said to Him, "Teacher, do You not care that we are perishing?" Then He arose and rebuked the wind, and said to the sea, "Peace, be still!" And the wind ceased and there was a great calm. But He said to them, "Why are you so fearful? How is it that you have no faith?" And they feared exceedingly, and said to one another, "Who can this be, that even the wind and the sea obey Him!" **Mark 4:35-41, NKJV**

On the door of my study, I have posted the following words by Rev. Charles Swindoll:

> The longer I live, the more I realize the impact of attitude on life. Attitude, to me, is more important than facts. It is more important than the past, than education, than money, than circumstances, than failures, than successes, than what other people think, say or do. It is more important than appearance, giftedness or skill. It will make or break a company . . . a church . . . a home. The remarkable thing is we have a choice every day regarding the attitude we embrace

for that day. We cannot change our past . . . we cannot change the fact that people will act in a certain way. We cannot change the inevitable. The only thing we can do is play the one string we have, and that is our attitude . . . I am convinced that life is 10% what happens to me and 90% how I react to it. And so it is with you . . . we are in charge of our attitudes.

I discovered these words many years ago on the wall of a restaurant in Charleston, South Carolina. These words are infinitely true because all of life is colored by attitude. An attitude is a perspective, a deliberate choice of perception, a state of mind. One looks at a glass of water and by way of attitude determines whether the glass is "half full" or "half empty." To say that the glass is half empty is to have a negative perspective, while to say that the glass is half full is to have a positive perspective. Too many people live life in the negative because of attitude. It was George Bernard Shaw who said, "Some look at life and ask, 'why?' I look at life as it ought to be and ask 'why not?'"

Deaconess Eva Crawford recently sent me a birthday card in which she wrote in her own hand an unusual, yet inspiring, line: "Rejoice, what a wonderful year it has been in the storm." She will never know what these words have meant to me. She was referring to the health challenges I have had to face, and rather than approach them from a negative and pessimistic perspective, Mrs. Crawford chose to refer to my last year as a "wonderful year in the storm."

To have "wonderful" and "storm" in the same sentence seems almost oxymoronic. They appear to be polar opposites. What is wonderful about a storm? Storms are destructive and often deadly.

How many people in New Orleans would refer to Hurricane Katrina as wonderful? How many people in New Jersey and New York would refer to Hurricane Sandy as wonderful? People who live with painful, terminal, and debilitating diseases would have a rough time referring to their disease or sickness as wonderful. However, it all has to do with attitude, perspective, one's choice of perception. The Christian believer stands with Mother Crawford because regardless of the strong circumstance or situation we stand with the Apostle Paul: "All things work together for good to them that love the Lord and the glory of His appearing."

It is the psalmist who places us in this same perspective when he says, "It was good for me to be afflicted, so that I might learn your decrees." (Psalm 119:71)

Our text from the Gospel of Mark speaks of "that day" or "the same day." There was a day when Jesus taught the parables of the Kingdom: the farm seeds, the growing seed, and the mustard seed. The teachings of Jesus must never be seen as simple platitudes or excesses in rhetoric. When Jesus teaches he does so with instruction for life; therefore, there must always be practical tests to see how much the disciples had learned. The storm in this text is part of that day's curriculum: What makes this or any storm wonderful?

The first words out of Jesus' mouth after a strenuous day of teaching were, "Let us go over to the other side." Before they embark upon this journey to the other side of the Sea of Galilee, Jesus says emphatically that they are going to the other side. He did not promise or say anything about an easy trip, but he did promise safe arrival to their destination. It did not matter that a storm would arise. The disciples had the assurance that they would cross the lake and arrive safely on the other side.

We must live with this same confidence. There is the confidence that we can rely on the promises of God. At the end of the day all we have are God's promises: "I will lead you by still waters; into green pastures; in the paths of righteousness." "Weeping may endure for a night, but joy cometh in the morning." "Yea, though I walk through the valley of the shadow of death I will fear no evil for thou are with me: Thy rod and thy staff comfort me." "He prepares a table in the presence of my enemy." "He will make every enemy a footstool."

In the midst of life's turbulence one must cling tenaciously to the belief that the Lord's promises are not empty rhetoric, but are real, concrete promises. I have every confidence that my Savior will safely navigate me through all of life's trials and vicissitudes.

> Standing on the promises that cannot fail,
>
> When the howling storms of doubt and fear assail,
>
> By the living Word of God I shall prevail,
>
> Standing on the promises of God!

I claim the storm as wonderful for a second reason: I have the Savior's presence. Not only do I have His promises, but I have His presence. The text does not say He sent them across the sea. He was in the boat with them. He had been teaching all day. Jesus is the Son of God, yes, but He was also human, and after teaching all day, He was exhausted. And so immediately when He got into the boat, He told them, "Let's push out to go to the other side." He fell asleep, and while He was asleep, the storm arose. The promise was, "We are going to the other side." Now the disciples not only have the promise, but they also have the presence of the Lord Himself in the boat.

The question is whether or not you believe the Lord is on board your ship. "Oh, I don't know what's going to happen now. I got some bad news. I really don't know what I'm going to do." Well, I thought you had Jesus. I mean, all this whooping and hollering you do on Sunday and all this hand clappin' and "Praise the Lord" you do on Sunday. Where is He in the storm? How do I translate that? How do I contemporize that today? Because Jesus never sleeps or slumbers. No, no, the Jesus I serve has ascended. He sits at the right hand of the Father, and He's not asleep. He's seated at the right hand of the Father with an assignment. It's a part of His destiny. He's seated at the right hand of the Father, making intercession for us. He's saying, "That's my child down there. There's a little bit of a storm. He or she has gotten some bad news, but I'm going to tell the Father, 'Watch over my child!'"

I have a Savior. Jesus knows all about my struggle. Does he know about yours? He shall guide until the day is done. There's not a friend like the lowly Jesus.

But the human part of Jesus is that he's tired in the text. He falls asleep in the boat. When the squall turns into a storm the Master is asleep. He sleeps in the confidence of his omniscience and omnipotence. He knows what will happen and He has the power to handle it!

Jesus' silence in a storm does not mean that He is absent in the storm. To wake Him up means to arouse our faith in Him. Our task is to awaken the faith we have in Him. He is on board our circumstance.

A statue of Rosa Parks was unveiled in the rotunda of the nation's capitol. It was this African American seamstress who refused to yield her seat on a segregated Montgomery, Alabama, bus in 1955 that galvanized the Black citizens of Montgomery, introduced Martin Luther King, Jr., and launched the Civil Rights Movement. On a day in 1955 when Rosa Parks was tired, coming home from work, she decided she wasn't going to move her seat. She looked at the driver who stopped the bus and said to her, "You're in the wrong section." And she said, "No, I'm not. Not today." And she said, "I'm in the right section because this is a seat. And I've been tired all day long. I'm a seamstress, and I'm not going to give up my seat." This was not the first time she had gotten on this bus, and it was not the first time she had encountered this particular bus driver. Several years ago, she had the same problem and he kicked her off the bus.

This Black woman would not give up her seat in the front of that Montgomery bus. Did she not consider her physical safety and well-being? She could have been beaten as well as killed. But Rosa Parks knew with undeniable certainty that she was not alone. She had the presence of the Lord Jesus Christ. How ironic, as House Speaker John Boehner said, that her statue would stand glancing at the statue of Jefferson Davis—President of the Confederacy—who lived and died wanting to keep slavery in place. Speaker Boehner said: "Look at her. She is surrounded by men who fought against everything she stood for." Every statue in the Rotunda is standing up, but the statue of Mother Parks has her sitting down. She sat down so that you and I can stand up! The presence of Jesus makes a difference.

There is a third consideration. This storm, and ours as well, is wonderful because we are granted license and liberty to question the Master about the storm. In the midst of the storm, Jesus was asleep. The disciples became fearful. They became afraid. They didn't hesitate. There's nowhere in the text that any disciple said to another disciple, "Let's not disturb him. You know he's tired. He's been teaching all day." They may have disagreed on stuff like seats, but way out in the middle of this storm, in unison, they woke him up and they asked him very pointedly: "Do you not care that we perish?"

Every storm is a teaching moment, and there can never be an authentic teaching moment without questions. The disciples were in unison on this. They did not conceal their questions, doubts, or fears. They verbalized this because they feared death.

It's a wonderful thing to know that no question is off-limits to God. He understands my humanity. He realizes that to question Him does not mean that I do not love Him. I question Him for clarity and assurance. You can't believe what grandmother taught on this subject. Grandmother was respectfully wrong when she said that one isn't supposed to question God. I contend that this is wrong because if she is right, then Jesus is a liar. Jesus said, "Ask and it shall be given." Since Jesus made this declaration, I do have the right to question God. I have license and liberty to question Him about anything, especially if it pertains to my welfare and my well-being. Job questioned Him: "O that I knew where I might find Him. I would fill my mouth with arguments and order my cares before Him." Thomas questioned Jesus about where He was going, and Jesus said, "I am the Way, the Truth, and the Life." Philip questioned Him about the Father, and Jesus said, "He that hath seen me hath seen the Father." Jesus questioned the Father: "My God! My God! Why hast Thou forsaken me?"

The African American slaves questioned God about their plight: "Lord, how come we here?" The Jews questioned God about their Egyptian oppression and the Holocaust. You and I are granted the same opportunity! We are expected to be honest about what we don't understand. We can raise our questions without pretense. What we must never forget is that only a storm can provoke certain questions. The comfort and conveniences of life will never produce the deep questions of our existence and soul. I cannot grow unless and until I raise my central questions. My questions reveal where I am in my faith journey. It is in the storm that my strengths and my weaknesses are revealed.

Finally, the storm is wonderful because it affords me the privilege to be an eyewitness to a miracle. You and I ought to live with expectations. We are to expect that God—at any moment—will break through my circumstance, break through my pain, break through my situation. I feel a breakthrough right now. It doesn't matter whether it's mine or yours. This week isn't going to be like last week. This year isn't going to be like last year, because I've got promises, presence, questions.

Jesus awakens from His sleep and wipes the cobwebs of slumber from His eyes. He yawns while the lightning is playing peekaboo in the dark. Thunder is creating all kinds of decibels. And the winds are howling. The waves are rocking the boat. And in the middle of the storm, Jesus says: "Peace, be still. Calm down. Lightning, I made you. Stop cracking. Thunder, I made you too. Shut up. Winds, I made you. Go back to your hiding place. Waves, as boisterous as you are, I made you too. Go to sleep on the bosom of my gentle command." Then he looked at the disciples and said, "Are you still afraid? Have you not yet learned? If I could open blind eyes, unstop deaf ears, put speech on dumb tongues, make lame folk throw away their crutches, and raise the dead, then wind, waves, lightning, and thunder—I can handle them, too."

Those twelve men became eyewitnesses to a miracle because they were in a wonderful storm. We cannot experience the supernatural when we don't expect the supernatural. When I sail on the ship of life with Jesus, I await the reality of the miraculous. I look for a miracle because I am a miracle and so are you! Make a change. Nobody's going to wave a wand over your situation. It's all about your attitude.

You know, you always run into these people who listen to you preach and they don't really listen because they've already thrown up a block. They say: "Well, all of that is fine, but . . ." Stop always putting in a "but" in your trying situations. There are no buts when it comes to God. Either you believe His promise or you don't. Either you believe His presence or you don't. Either you have the courage to raise the questions or you don't. Either you believe in the possibility of a miracle or a breakthrough or you don't. There are no buts!

He's the same God who stilled the storm then, and He'll still your storm now. Your pain isn't any different than somebody else's pain. Your circumstance is no different. You have every opportunity to change your attitude just like I have to change mine. Just because I'm a preacher does not mean that I have some special dispensation of grace. What's available to me is available to you too.

A couple of weeks ago I was in a meeting. A gentleman kept looking at me. When the meeting adjourned, he made haste and came to me. And he said, "I hear you have been sick." I said, "I'm doing all right." He said, "Yeah, but, I heard you been having some trouble." So by this time he was getting on my last nerve. I said, "I'm doing fine. I'm doing fine." He said, "Yeah, but I heard you ain't been well." What he wanted me to do was start talking about the issue, and finally when I couldn't take it anymore, I looked at him and put my hand on my hip and said, "Well, how do I look?" That's what you have to tell people. You don't need to give an explanation of what you're going through. You ought to be a visible sign that God's taking care of you. All one needs to say is, "I don't look like what I'm going through."

We need to thank God for the wonderful time in the storm. I thank God today that the storm is not controlling me. I'm controlling the storm. So right now, in the name of Jesus, I pray for attitudes. I pray for a change of attitudes. Somebody needs to know we're not victims, but we are soldiers. Soldiers take a lickin', but they keep on tickin'. Thank you, Father, for the possibility of breakthrough. We are waiting on you for our miracle in the midst of the storm. In fact, the beginning of the breakthrough starts now with my attitude. With all I'm going through, I need to stop right now and say, "It could be a whole lot worse."

I pray that you have the courage to stand on God's promises, that you have the courage to stand in God's presence. I pray that you have the courage to raise the questions in the storm, and that you believe that a miracle is on the way. In fact, truth be told, we're a miracle right now. I should have been dead, but I'm here now. My boat should've capsized a long time ago. So I'm going to have a wonderful time in the middle of this storm!

THE GLORY SPOT

Again they tried to seize him, but he escaped their grasp. Then Jesus went back across the Jordan to the place where John had been baptizing in the early days. There he stayed and many people came to him. They said, "Though John never performed a miraculous sign, all that John said about this man was true." And in that place many believed in Jesus. **John 10:39-42, NIV**

In the 18th century there lived a great composer by the name of George Frideric Handel. Anyone who is at all familiar with church music knows that this is a name that towers above many. When I think about George Frideric Handel, I think about what Jesus said when he declared that many are called, but few are chosen. And in my opinion, George Frideric Handel stands heads and shoulders above many who have composed great music.

It is said of George Frideric Handel that there came a period in his life when he was at his lowest. He found his life invaded by creditors who were knocking at his door. Handel could barely pay his rent. In many instances it was difficult for him to even eat on a daily basis. Yet, with all of these negative circumstances, there was something in him that allowed him to believe that somehow, some way, he would emerge from this dark season unscathed.

All of us have what I call "dull moments" in life. We have those moments when it seems as if the sun does not shine, and even though it does shine it's as if it does not shine completely on us. And there are times when we do find ourselves between a rock and a hard place, between the devil and the deep blue sea. And if we're honest enough, we will confess that there are times when we wonder if God has forgotten where we live. Are there not questions in your life that He has not answered? Are there not problems in your life that He has not solved? Are there not seasons that appear darkened by negative circumstances and draining experiences until you wonder where is the goodness of God in my life?

What is ultimately awesome about the God whom we serve is that sometimes when we are at our lowest we discover God at his best. This is why it could be implied that anyone who commits suicide does not give God the chance to stick His hand into the darkness of what you consider to be an impossibility and bring out a possibility.

Many would consider it a tragedy that someone would reach such a nadir moment in his life that he would consider life no longer worth living. Perhaps he had a myriad of health problems and he did not know how to deal with them, and rather than trust God with those difficulties, he prematurely ended his life.

My friend Walter Thomas often speaks of those moments in life when we feel lower than a footprint. George Frideric Handel reached such a moment. He locked himself in his apartment. People would knock on his door, and he refused to answer. And for a number of successive days, nobody knew what he was doing, and they wondered whether or not he had, in fact, lost his mind. He had not lost his mind at all, but God had turned his living quarters into a glory spot. For during those days when Handel did not speak to a soul, he was composing what I consider to be the single greatest piece of music ever written by a human being: Handel's *Messiah*.

Would you not agree that it is passionately refreshing how that wonderful piece of music ends with the Hallelujah chorus, where we are reminded that Jesus is "King of kings and Lord of lords and he shall reign forever and ever and of his kingdom there shall be no end"? What makes that particular piece of music so great is that every word of it is scripture. There is not one human word beyond what is recorded in sacred scripture. It is said that when Handel opened the door, tears were flowing from his eyes. Those who gazed upon him said they saw "at that moment upon him the glory of God."

What is the glory of God? The glory of God is the indwelling of God's Spirit. What is the glory of God? The glory of God is the venerable manifestation of God's presence. Whenever you are in the presence of the Lord, people ought to know it. When Moses descended the mountain of Sinai after receiving the tablets of stone upon which were written the Law of God, his face radiated with the presence of God and people knew that he had been with the Lord. In the New Testament, when you read portions of the Acts of the Apostles, particularly when Peter and John are brought before the Sanhedrin after healing the man who was crippled at the gate called Beautiful, the enemies of the Church took notice of those common men, Peter and John, and Luke says in the book of Acts that they took note that these men had been with Jesus.

The question we all must ask ourselves is, When others look at us, is it easy to discern that we have been in the presence of God? The presence of God is not some evasive something, but the presence of God is an enveloping something. It is an all-consuming something. Is it not the writer of Hebrews who says that our God is a consuming fire?

Well, if God is a consuming fire, there ought to at least be some smoke coming from one in whom God's presence resides. Even if there are no flames, even if there are no embers, there ought to be some smoke emanating from your life. There ought to be something that oozes out of your personality that lets people know that there is something divine about you—not superior, not better, but simply that the presence of God is alive and active in your life.

In the focal text for this sermon, Jesus has gone into the temple of Solomon, envisioned originally by David but built by his son, Solomon. Jesus now walks in that portion of the temple known as Solomon's Colonnade. He is there for a particular reason and purpose, that being to celebrate the Feast of Dedication, or what is referred to today as "Hanukkah." It represented the purifying of the temple by Judas Maccabeus in 165 BC, after Antiochus Epiphanes had desecrated the temple by sacrificing a pig on the altar of burnt offering. It was one of the high festive religious days for the Jews, and yet the enemies of Jesus accost him, and they really want to know pointedly, "Are you the Son of God?"

What draws one to this text is that this is one moment in which Jesus decides not to be mild. We like to talk about "be like the Lord; be meek and mild," but the Lord wasn't always meek and mild. That day when He drove the money-changers out of the Temple with leather whips, it would be a stretch to define these actions as meek or mild.

"Are you the Son of God?" they ask. And Jesus looks at them and says, "Have I not told you before that I am the Son of God? Have I not performed for you miraculous signs?" John the Baptist never performed one miracle. John preached. John preached that the ax was laid at the root of the tree. John referred to his generation as a brood of vipers. John baptized, but John never performed a miracle. Jesus has performed many miracles and thus looks at His adversaries and says, "I've told you who I am."

How many of you know what it is to say what you really feel when people get on your last nerve? It's kind of like when your mother told you to do something over and over again, then finally she comes to you and says, "I'm not going to tell you that anymore." Her voice rises. You can tell by the tempo and the timbre of her voice the serious intent of her statements.

Jesus says, in effect, "I'm not up for any foolishness this day." And then He says bluntly, "I am the Son of God." The tension is here revealed. They ask Him if He's the Son of God. He tells them pointedly that He is the Son of God, and when He says it, they accuse Him of blasphemy. And the Bible says, according to John, that they tried to seize Him. God, however, provides a way of escape for Jesus as He does for others at times when we are obeying His will.

Many people carry a testimony that there were times when the enemy almost seemed to have prevailed. It is often in those seasons when God provides avenues of escape. It could be interpreted that God will allow the enemy to come only so close to a follower's life. Perhaps this could be one of the interpretations of the scripture that says "no weapon formed against me shall prosper." Look at what Jesus does. He retreats across the Jordan by Himself apart from His disciples, to the place where John baptized Jesus and others in the early days of Jesus' ministry. Jesus used this spot as His "glory spot."

We all need a place where there is no doubt that God is in residence. Everybody ought to have a glory spot. Everybody ought to have a place where you know the presence of the Lord dwells. In fact, it might be implied that one can have many glory spots.

But this is a particular glory spot, because it was in the Jordan Valley, where Jesus was baptized by John. Jesus remembered when John said,

"I'm not worthy to even stoop and undo the latchet on your shoes."
But Jesus responded, "Suffer it to be so now." Jesus never baptized
anybody, but He Himself was baptized. He was not sprinkled; He was
immersed. He was placed down in the water so that His whole body
was submerged.

Jesus got baptized not because He was sinful, not because there was
any fault or failure, but He did it as a symbol and sign to the rest of us
that if we are to follow Him, we are to lay to rest the old human being
and come up a new creation. You know what happened when Jesus was
baptized? The heavens opened up. God descended like a dove, hovered
over His Son, and then God Himself spoke. God echoed from eternity,
"This is my beloved Son, in whom I am well pleased."

Jesus' returning to this spot is almost a way of saying, "Now that
my enemies are on my trail and I'm headed towards that which will
culminate in my death, I need a glory spot. I need a place where I can
remember how good God has been." How sad it would be for one to
reach a dark moment in life and not have a glory spot.

Why does Jesus go to this place? Why is this place a glory spot? It's
not a temple. It's not a synagogue. There's nothing ornate about it. It's
just a place out near the Jordan Valley. But it has meaning and purpose
for Him. It was here in this glory spot that Jesus heard the voice of His
Father and got direction for the rest of His earthly journey. And you
and I need to return to glory spots so that we can hear the voice of God
and determine what God's direction is for our lives.

This is important because sometimes one's direction changes.
When Jesus came to the Jordan Valley to be baptized by John, He came
as a carpenter. He was in his earthly father's profession. By this time,
Jesus was 30 years of age, and we believe that Joseph was dead. Jesus

had been serving as the primary breadwinner for the family, but now God says, "This is my Son, in whom I am well pleased. It's time for you now to make a career change. For the last few years, you've been a carpenter. That's on your earthly father's side. But you didn't come into the world to be a carpenter. I made you to do something more than make tables, chairs, and doors. When you were born, I told your mother and earthly father, 'And thou shall call his name "Jesus," for he shall save his people from their sins.' It's time now to make your transition from carpenter to messiah."

Going back to the "glory spot" could be for confirming spiritual direction. The "glory spot" could reestablish what has been expressed in prayers, pondered in meditation, and heard through preaching.

Jesus goes to the Jordan Valley and shuts the door forever on the carpenter's shop. The assumption is that He already has made plans for taking care of His mother, because now He assumes a role that will no longer allow Him to be the primary breadwinner in the family. It's time for Him to begin His itinerant ministry. It could be suggested that when God shifts one's life in a new direction, God will make one go places that are unconventional and inconvenient.

For example, look at where Jesus goes after His baptism. Immediately after hearing God say, "This is my beloved Son," Jesus is led straight into the wilderness, of all places. He's not driven by the devil. He's not driven by his ego. He's driven by His Father into the wilderness of Gethsemane, where in 40 days He is tempted three different times.

The devil tells him, "First turn these stones into bread." But Jesus says, "No. Man shall not live by bread alone." The adversary takes Him to the pinnacle of the temple. "Cast yourself down, for it says in the 91st Psalm that he will give his angels charge over thee." But Jesus says, "No.

Thou shalt not tempt the Lord thy God." Finally, the devil takes him to the highest pinnacle in all of the earth, shows Him all of the kingdoms of the world, and says, "They shall be yours if you bow down." Jesus says to him, "I worship God and God alone."

When was the last time you heard God's voice? When was the last time He spoke to you? Because when God speaks, God can guide you around certain things as well as guide you away from certain people. You think about so many people who are suffering in the cycle of drug addiction. Many of them didn't just determinedly enter into the drug world. Somebody tempted them by asking perhaps, "Have you tried this?" Part of faith is knowing when to express to God, "Hold my hand."

Whenever I go back to Baltimore, I go back to my glory spot. My glory spot is not 1936 West Lanvale Street. My glory spot is not my mother's grave. But my glory spot is a church on the corner of Edmonson Avenue and Schroeder Street, where I first heard the name of the Lord. That's where I was baptized. That's where I was licensed and ordained to preach the Gospel. Everybody ought to have a glory spot.

The glory spot is not just a place where you hear God's voice and you get God's direction. The glory spot in the text represents a place where Jesus could get a respite from his enemies. As perfect as Jesus was, as faultless as He was, His enemies got on His nerves. There is comfort in reading this because it reflects the experiences we all have even as disciples of the Lord's. One of the honest realities of living as a disciple of Christ is having to incarnate Jesus' want for us to "Love your enemies, and to do good to them who hate us."

Jesus had crossed the Jordan to get rest from His enemies. If He had wanted to challenge them, He could have. But God said, "Not today. There isn't going to be a debate today, no dialog today, not today. Today you're going to retreat because you need a rest from your enemies."

The glory spot is where I hear His voice and get direction. The glory spot is where I get a respite from my enemies. And the glory spot is the place where we get encouragement, incentive, and inspiration for what's ahead. Because with all of our intellect and with all of our abilities, with all of the gifts and resources we possess, we cannot predict the future.

There were three things that Jesus had to deal with. First, He had to get away from His enemies. Second, He had to deal with knowing what was ahead of Him across the Jordan in the next chapter in Bethany. Whenever you hear "Bethany," you ought to think of Lazarus, Mary, and Martha. Lazarus was sick. But despite Jesus' tight relationship with Lazarus, Mary, and Martha, Jesus did not drop what He was doing. And when you read in the next chapter around the sixth verse, it says that He stayed where he was two more days.

Now we know where He was for those two days: He was at His glory spot getting what He needed to raise Lazarus from the dead. There are times when you must be inaccessible, even to your family and your friends, because God is giving you strength. God is giving you impetus. God is giving you inspiration and encouragement to handle stuff up the road that you cannot yet define because you cannot yet see it.

When Jesus finally shows up two days later, Martha says, "If you had been here, our brother would not have died." Jesus, freshly refueled from His time in the glory spot, quickly responded, "Show me where you laid him."

Isn't that the blessed extension of grace given to all of us in relationship with Jesus, where to us He says, "Show me where you laid him"? "Show me your trouble. Show me your trial. Show me your tribulation. Show me your sickness. I got power to raise the dead."

"Show me your slavery. Show me your middle passage. Show me reconstruction. Show me your black coals. Show me the Ku Klux Klan. Show me the white citizens' council. Show me racism, and I'll show you how far I can bring you. Show me how they tortured Emmett Till. Show me what they did to those Black girls in Birmingham. Show me your grief, and when the smoke clears and the dust settles, I'll have a Black man in the White House. Show me."

God gives Jesus what He needs at the glory spot because in Bethany He needed resurrection power for Lazarus. But there was a third hurdle He had to clear. He raised Lazarus, but He was getting ready to die.

Jesus needed the glory spot because He knew what was up the road. He knew that betrayal was up the road. He knew that abandonment was up the road. He knew that denial was up the road. He knew that nails were up the road. He knew that a spike was up the road. He knew that a platted crown of thorns was up the road. He knew that a pointed tip of the spear was up the road, and He needed power to handle what was up the road. And let's not forget that in that moment of needing power, even though He had been to the glory spot, there was still that moment when He felt abandoned.

The glory spot is where I hear the Master's voice and get direction. The glory spot is where I get a respite from my enemies. The good news is that the glory spot will always give you encouragement, incentive, and inspiration for what's ahead. It's a gift of God to prepare you for the great work of Kingdom expansion as you become a tool in the Master's hand!

THE IMPOSSIBILITY OF DEFEAT

When you go to war against your enemies and see horses and chariots and an army greater than yours, do not be afraid of them, because the LORD your God, who brought you up out of Egypt, will be with you. When you are about to go into battle, the priest shall come forward and address the army. He shall say: "Hear, O Israel, today you are going into battle against your enemies. Do not be fainthearted or afraid; do not be terrified or give way to panic before them. For the LORD your God is the one who goes with you to fight for you against your enemies to give you victory."
Deuteronomy 20:1-4, NIV

It is quite unfortunate that there are people in the world who live for a great number of years but fail to understand the reality of this mystery that we call life. There are those who think that because they have lived a certain number of years, and because of their experiences, they have a grip on life. But if I understand anything at all about life, I understand this much: Life is, has been, and always will be unpredictable. It does not matter whether you are a saint or a sinner, whether you are in or out of the church, life is an unpredictable sojourn.

Our mothers and our fathers referred to life as an uneven journey. And they would say life is sometimes up, sometimes down, sometimes almost level to the ground. I have been disturbed over the last several years as I've listened to preachers and as I've read contemporary literature of faith that there are people who honestly believe and have so hypnotized themselves to think that life can be lived with the absence of conflict. I do not believe that for one minute.

Live is a dialectical experience. In all of life, there is a dialectic, there is a tension between what is good and bad, what is right and what is wrong, what is righteous and what is wicked. In *Time* magazine there was a story about our president, and I was disturbed by a comment he made. Mr. Obama said, "When I am elected, my antagonists, my nemeses, my enemies across the aisle, will come and line up behind me because they will have seen the marked difference between who I am and what I represent in comparison to my opponents. They will step in line and fall in sync and begin to support the many things that they have been against." I thought to myself, "Either he's being politically kind or he is extremely naïve." Given the intelligent man that he is, there's no way that I can believe he really means that because the argument against him is not so much political as it's racial. Everything that he has sought to do has been for the betterment of all people; yet, there are those who are against him, I believe, simply for ethnic reasons, for racial reasons. I listen to the venom with which his enemies speak, how even now, after all these years, they still want to raise questions about his birth status.

I encourage us to understand that he is in a battle, a war. It's not just a political conflict. This is a dialectical tension between what I believe is good and evil, right and wrong. Paul said, "What do righteousness and wickedness have in common? What fellowship can there be between light and darkness?" Paul put it another way when he said, "Our battle is not against flesh and blood, but our battle is against principalities, our battle is against powers. Our battle is against the rulers of darkness in high places and spiritual wickedness as well." I love William Jefferson

Clinton. He stood on the stage of the Democratic National Convention and said, "I do not understand the venom of my opponents, how they can speak with such hatred." And then he threw his hands up. He said, "You impeached me. You voted me out or at least tried to. And yet I don't hate you for what you have done."

And it really takes a strong Christian to look at people who you know mean you ill, and yet declare, "I love you anyhow." As long as you and I live, there will always be a dialectical tension between what is good and what is bad. Condoleezza Rice, the former secretary of state underneath President George Bush, said something that I really believe. And don't misunderstand me—I'm not a pessimist; I'm a realist. I do not believe that racism will ever be eradicated from this country. I don't believe it ever will. Condoleezza Rice is right when she said that racism "is America's original birth defect."

Racism is woven into the fabric of what this country is all about, and as much as we try, and we should always try, there's always this tension between black and white. We talk about how God-fearing the country is, but nobody talks about the fact that after all of these years following the Emancipation Proclamation the nation has never apologized for slavery. No one has ever erased that part of the Constitution that would define somebody who looks like me as three-fifths of a human being. I am not three-fifths of a human being. I am made in the image of God and created after His likeness.

I don't stand on the Declaration of Independence. I don't stand on the Constitution. I stand on the Word of the Living God, and the Word of the Living God says that I am made in His image, created after His likeness. There is a tension, always, between good and evil, right and wrong. The issue becomes are you more patriotic than you are God-fearing? I don't love the flag so much that I put it above the Word of God. Heaven and earth shall pass away, but the Word of the Lord shall stand forever. In our text Moses is somewhere between 60 and 120 years of age, but his mind is clear as a bell. As he stands before the people of Israel who are about to embark upon the taking of the promised land, a land that is already occupied, and a land, therefore, that must be overtaken. He pulls no punches with the people of Israel. He gives a directive. He gives a command from God, and the command is this: "If you are going to occupy the land that I promised long ago to Abraham, to Isaac and Jacob; if it is, in fact, the patriarchal promise that I have given to you, then the land must be overtaken, and the land must be fought for."

The Christian faith is not a punk faith. It's not a weak faith. It's not something that we simply embrace on Sunday morning and then leave alone for the other six days of the week. The Christian faith is a faith that is to be lived. If we are to live it, then it would seem sometimes that there must be a struggle and a fight, since we live in conflict. Augustine wrote a wonderful work entitled *The City of God*, in which he defines Christians as resident aliens, meaning that I am a resident in this world, but I am an alien because, ultimately, my citizenship belongs to another commonwealth.

My mother put it this way: "This old world ain't my home." It is because I am a resident alien, every now and then the values of my ultimate home fall into conflict with the values of this world. Anybody who understands the beam of the Judeo-Christian ethic understands that God gives us the right and the permission to fight for something. A lot of folk don't want to agree with me, but if we're going to get our community back and away from the drug lords and the gangbangers, we're going to have to fight for it.

Have you forgotten the words of the 15th Chapter of Exodus when the children of Israel marched through on dry land, when God brings them through the Sea of Reeds or what we call the Red Sea, and Miriam banged on that tambourine and Moses sang? And what did Moses sing? Moses sang a war song: "The horse and the rider he hath thrown into the sea. Our God is a man of war, and the Lord is His name." Where would be today as a people if Martin King didn't fight, if John Lewis didn't fight, if Malcolm didn't fight, if A. Philip Randolph didn't fight?

No, I'm not talking about guns and knives. I'm not talking about the physicality of war. I'm talking about the mindset of war. We shall not roll over and let the devil have his way in our lives. Do you have something or somebody worth fighting for? You ought to be willing to fight for your children and fight for this community and fight for our values. I don't believe that we ought to roll over and play dead and act as if God's just going to do things in His own time.

That's why He saved us. That's why He has empowered us. That's why He has enabled us.

> Am I a soldier of the cross, a follower of the Lamb,
> and shall I fear to own His cause, or blush to speak His
> name? Must I be carried to the skies on flowery beds
> of ease, while others fought to win the prize, and sailed
> through bloody seas?"

I love the third verse: "Sure I must fight, if I would reign; increase"— here it is—"my courage, Lord." And if you do that, "I'll bear the toil." If you do that, I'll "endure the pain," as long as I am "supported by thy word."

I'm sorry, but I'm not one of these new-day preachers who wants to talk about how good things are. They are good, but only to an extent. Someone has to tell the truth. We've come a long way, but we have a long way to go. It would seem to me that we ought to fight for what we believe. I don't believe for one minute that Christians are defeated people. We fail, yes, because we are human, we are mortal, and we have finitude. We have setbacks, yes, because we stumble and fall. But defeated? Not at all!

This is not a defeatist declaration: "I can do all things through Jesus Christ who strengthens me." Neither is, "Greater is He that is in me than he that is in the world," or "No weapon, however strong, formed against me shall prosper." These are not the words of a defeatist. These are the words of folk who win against devastating odds.

What gives me the right to stand before you today and declare that if you are a child of God, it is impossible for you to be defeated? The text says,

> When you go to war against your enemies and see horses and chariots and an army greater than yours"—when you get ready to battle and discover that the forces are greater than what you are—"do not be afraid of them, because the LORD your God, who brought you up out of Egypt, will be with you.

In other words, defeat is impossible when I recognize that whenever I get into a battle the Lord is with me. Moses reminds the Israelites that there was no greater victory in Israel than the victory that God gave them when He brought them up out of the land of Egypt, up out of the land of oppression after 400 years of slavery. He said, "Whatever you come up against, remember that you already have a victory in your trophy case."

Most of us lose battles because we lose the battle in the mind. Every battle that you fight begins in your head. You win or lose your battle based upon how you think. Paul said, "Let this mind be in you that was in Christ Jesus." If God could bring His people out of slavery, if God could bring them up out of oppression, if God could bring them up out of bondage, what do you think He can do with your battle now?

Notice the text; it says, "When you go..." War is inevitable. Notice that he does not speak in the singular, but he speaks in the plural. He says, "When you go to war against your enemy...," meaning that you're going to have enemies. Not just today, but always. Anybody who stands up for what the Lord says, is going to have enemy after enemy after enemy. The giants keep on coming.

Somebody wondered why God had David pick up five smooth stones when he only needed one to bring down Goliath. This was just in case Goliath had some brothers or some cousins.This was God's way of saying, "I have a rock for them, too."

At the end of the day, all Israel had was God. They had no weapons because they were slaves, but God brought them out. Pharaoh had horses and chariots. Pharaoh had swords and spears. Pharaoh had the mightiest military machine at that time known to humanity, but he lost because Israel had Somebody mightier than horses and chariots. Israel had Somebody mightier than swords and spears. When God decided to go to battle for Israel, God started using everything He made. He used gnats, flies, hail, boils, blood, locusts, and plagues. And then He used the death angel. When you have God, you have everything. When you have God on your side, you have creation on your side.

Now if anybody ought to know that, Black folk ought to know.
We ought to know because at the end of the day all we've had is God.
We were slaves. The judiciary was against us. The legislative branch
of government was against us; the executive branch was against us.
However, we had God.

And some still don't want to shout. After all we've been through,
we still have joy." "I don't know how I'm going to get that house out
of foreclosure, but I have God." "I don't know how I'm going to raise
my child as a single parent, but I have God." "I don't know how we are
going to make it with Congress voting down everything the man tries
to put up, but we have God." God has gone up against worse.

I can't lose because I have on the helmet of salvation. I can't lose
because I've have on the breastplate of righteousness. I can't lose because
I have on the girdle of truth. I can't lose because I have on the sandals of
peace. I can't lose because I've got the shield of faith. I can't lose because I
have the sword of the Spirit. Glory to God. The sword of the Spirit, which
is the Word of the living God.

Look at what else the text says:

> When you are about to go into battle, the priest shall
> come forward, and the priest shall address the army.
> And the priest shall say: 'Hear, Oh Israel: Today you
> are going into battle against your enemies. But do not
> be fainthearted. Don't be afraid; do not terrified and
> do not give way to panic.'

It is impossible for me to be defeated because I have an eternal word of
encouragement and inspiration.

Israel never went into battle without first getting a directive from the
priest. The directive is, "Do not be afraid; do not be fainthearted; don't

be terrified. And whatever you do, don't panic." Life is beating you up, killing you. You need somebody to stand up there and tell you, "Let not your heart be troubled." You need somebody to tell you, "Everything is going to be all right." You need somebody to tell you that God said, "I will never leave you. I will never forsake you."

The text says, "When you are about to go into battle, the priest shall come forward, and the priest shall address the army." The Lord isn't talking to folk who won't fight. The Word of the Lord is for folk who are ready to fight. If you don't have any fight in you, then I'm not talking to you. I don't have a word for you. But I have a word for folk who are going up against the devil. I have a word for folk who are going up against obstacles and stumbling blocks. The word from the priest is only for the army—the fighting folk.

So that means if you're going to fight in the army, you have to fight against your obstacles and stumbling blocks first. You have to win the battle in your mind. Every battle that you win or lose, you lose in your mind or you win in your mind first. The Lord has a word for folk who fight. He doesn't have a word for cowards. He doesn't have a word for folk who roll over and play dead.

Nebuchadnezzar put Shadrach, Meshach, and Abednego in that fiery furnace. When he looked in the fiery furnace and saw the fourth man, what did he cry out? He cried, "Oh, praise the God of Shadrach, Meshach, and Abednego." When Darius, king of the Medes, put Daniel in the lions' den, and saw the lion—that Daniel was asleep on the lion's back, he said, "Oh, praise the God of Daniel and may he live forever." The word is for the people who fight. Fighters are encouraged, fighters are inspired.

I can't be defeated because I have a mammoth victory or victories in my trophy case; I have something I can already look back on. I cannot be defeated because God always sends me a mouthpiece in the church, who inspires and encourages me against all odds. But here's what I love. Moses said—and notice how personal he is—"For the Lord, *your* God is the one who goes with *you* to fight for *you* against *your* enemies to give *you* victory."

"For the Lord, *your* God is the one who goes with *you* to fight for *you* against *your* enemies to give you victory."

How can I be defeated, when in the language of Martin King, "I have cosmic companionship"? I have cosmic companionship. You can't see them, but in the atmosphere right now are angels. And above those angels is a God who is my Creator. And inside of me is a Savior who redeemed me one day. And pushing me is the impetus of the *Hagios Pneuma*, the Holy Ghost. I have cosmic companionship.

God is able to do exceedingly and abundantly above anything that we can think or dream. He will fight for us. You got that loan because God fought for you. Somebody else was supposed to get that job, but God fought for you. You got that house out of foreclosure because God fought for you. Some stuff you have that your gift and your training did not get you; God opened that door, God made the way. The Book said that not only is He with me, not only will He fight, but He'll give me victory.

Well, if God is on my side, and if God is fighting for me, and if God has promised to give me victory, then how can I lose? I may be bloody, I may be battered, but at the end of the day I'm going to raise my hand and declare that victory is mine. I told Satan, "Get behind." I told Satan, "Get thee behind because victory is mine." How many of you believe there's a hell somewhere? How many of you believe that there is hell in this world? How many of you have lived in hell?

How many of you are witnesses and can say, "I've been to hell and back"? Depression is hell. Disappointment is hell. Racism is hell. Sexism is hell. Classism is hell. And to all hell, I say no! Somebody ought to be able to say, "Hell, no!" When it comes to my demise, hell, no! When it comes to my depression, hell, no! When it comes to my frustration, hell, no! When somebody tries to put me down, hell, no! When you cuss me and think you're going to break my spirit, hell, no!

Because hell is the antithesis of heaven, I say no to anything that looks like hell. I say hell, no! To everything that's chaotic. I say hell, no! to everything that is confusing. If God is for me, that's better than the whole world against me.

How do you overcome hell and tell hell no? It's in the Revelation. They overcame hell by the blood of the Lamb and by the light of their testimony. Two things you can't argue with me about: One is the blood of the Lamb and the second one is my testimony. I have a testimony. This is my story! This is my song! I'm praising my Savior, not just on Sunday, but all the day long.

THERE IS ALWAYS
SOMETHING LEFT TO LOVE

"Meanwhile the older son was in the field. When he came near the house he heard music and dancing. So he called one of his servants and asked him what was going on. 'Your brother has come,' he replied, 'and your father has killed the fattened calf because he has him back safe and sound.' The older brother became angry and refused to go in. So his father went out and pleaded with him. But he answered his father, 'Look! All these years I've been slaving for you and never disobeyed your orders. Yet you never gave me even a young goat so I could celebrate with my friends. But when this son of yours who has squandered your property with prostitutes comes home, you kill the fattened calf for him!' 'My son,' the father said, 'you are always with me, and everything I have is yours. But we had to celebrate and be glad, because this brother of yours was dead and is alive again; he was lost and is found.'" **Luke 15:25-32, NIV**

One of the greatest plays ever written by an African American, in my opinion, is Lorraine Hansberry's "A Raisin in the Sun," which originally debuted on Broadway in 1959. More recently, it was staged again starring Sean "P. Diddy" Combs, Phylicia Rashad, Sanaa Lathan, and the gifted actress and vocalist Audra McDonald. Fifty years ago, Sydney Poitier, Ruby Dee, and Claudia McNeil were responsible for the starring roles.

Those familiar with Hansberry's masterpiece will recall that toward the play's conclusion the mother of the Younger clan has purchased a house. Walter Lee, the son, was responsible for making sure the money for the house was properly deposited so that when needed, it could be secured. But Walter Lee squanders the money in a get-rich-quick scheme with his friends, who eventually disappear with the money.

When the reality of this scheme comes to light, Walter Lee is embarrassed because he had been entrusted with money that would change their lives and their futures. When his sister, Beneatha, finds out the money is gone, she goes on a tirade. She tells him he is irresponsible. She tells him of her embarrassment and humiliation and that she no longer considers him to be her brother. Beneatha does not realize her mother overheard what was said. When Beneatha was through, the mother says, "Everything you've said is right. Your brother is irresponsible and that which he has done is embarrassing and humiliating. But never allow yourself to ever come to the place where you disown your own flesh and blood. Regardless of what he has done, still in Walter Lee, there is something left to be loved."

I was so moved by that one poignant line: "There is always something left to be loved." Immediately, the Holy Spirit laid on my heart the parable of the prodigal son—"prodigal" meaning wasteful. We know from Scripture this familiar story of how the prodigal son demanded his inheritance from his father, and without argument, debate, dialogue, or discussion, the father gave the son what was his. With inheritance in hand, the son goes into a far country, squanders it in riotous living, and is forced to live under Gentile dominion in the midst of hogs. When he reaches that nadir point, which is the lowest point of human existence, "he comes to his senses." Then he says, "How many servants does my father have? I'm not used to living like this. I will arise, go to my father and tell my father that I've sinned against heaven and against him. I'm no more worthy to be called his son. I will ask him to make me as one of his hired hands" (Luke 15:17-19).

Despite shame, the prodigal son makes his way home. The father sees him in the distance and immediately runs to him, kisses him, and calls for a celebration. A fattened calf is killed. A ring is placed back on his finger. A golden robe is placed upon his shoulders and sandals upon his feet, and then the father says, "My son who was lost is now found; this boy who was dead is now made alive" (Luke 15:32).

Had the parable ended at the point of celebration, it would have been a wonderful and simple story. But Jesus is such a stark realist and concludes the story by bringing in the older brother to center stage. Sibling drama—many of us know that particular pain all to well. The elder brother in this tale represents those of us who are pharisaic and love to receive mercy, but have a difficult time extending it. The younger brother has lived life foolishly and made tragic mistakes—and who has not? When it comes to the moment of his return and restoration, his father celebrates, but his only sibling is disturbed and angry and will not embrace his prodigal brother.

Many of us are seasoned enough and wise enough to know not everyone is thrilled when we return to sanity. Not everyone will celebrate our restoration, healing, and homecoming. In my opinion, one of the great tragedies as a people is that we don't celebrate each other or praise each other enough for our accomplishments. Far too often our jealousies and insecurities get in the way. As pastors and parishioners, when someone walks into the sanctuary, we should not be more concerned about what they have done or where they have been than about with our willingness to love them. We should be praising God that they are in the building. When someone is presented as a candidate for baptism, we ought not judge each other and question their motives. We ought to celebrate that they are coming to the One who can wash away all their sins. We ought to celebrate their new life in Christ. Here's the bottom line: the reality is that all of us have emerged from something of our past and deserve restoration.

And so did this son of the Bible who lost his way. But the elder brother says to his father, "You never had a celebration or a party for me. You've never fattened a calf for me, not even a goat. I never caused you trouble. I never caused you any embarrassment. I studied and never brought shame on the family. I've been with you all my life. I've lived by the rules, and yet that son of yours has wasted his inheritance, squandered his living, and has been with prostitutes. Now you kill the fattened calf for him, dress him with robes, place a ring upon his finger and sandals on his feet." The elder brother does not say, "My brother"; he calls him his father's son. Then the father says, "If you had good sense, you would rejoice as well."

Some of us have been in the church so long and been holy so long that we have developed a convenient form of amnesia. We've forgotten that somebody prayed for us. We have forgotten that somebody kept us on their mind. Somebody has even forgiven us when we have acted complete fools. Haven't we all fallen short of the glory of God and done something insipidly stupid? We all have made bad choices and awakened the next day to face both ourselves and our deeds. But somebody prayed for us anyway. We all have been there and we all have a story to tell, or one to keep secret. But thank God even if nobody witnessed our misdeeds, God still says there's always something left to love.

The father in the Scripture is a mature man and has a perspective on his younger son's return that his elder son, who is immature, does not. The father understood that his younger son did not allow sin to destroy his being. Sin will always dissipate—dissipation meaning "to diminish."

Sin diminishes and takes away from one's character and robs one of value and virtue. So the father runs to meet his younger son, knowing his son had enough wisdom to realize that "I may be diminished, I may be dissipated, but I am not destroyed." That is something to shout about. God can rescue us from our far-off countries and give us the strength to look the devil in the eye and say, "I've made some mistakes, but I will not be diminished. I will not be destroyed." Dissipation does not have to mean destruction. When the young man comes to his senses, the father recognizes that he is repentant and has changed.

Luke 15 is about being lost and found, and it begins with the sheep that wanders away because of foolishness. Next is the parable of the lost coin, which deals with carelessness and a coin that has been lost in daylight. But in the parable of the prodigal son, there is more than foolishness, there is more than carelessness, and there is loss because of willfulness. The younger son was willful and relied on his own understanding. Our most difficult times often come when we start to rely solely on ourselves. "Trust in the LORD with all your heart and lean not on your own understanding; in all your ways acknowledge him, and he will make your paths straight" (Proverbs 3:5-6, NIV).

Many ministers no longer want to examine the issue and implications of sin, but sin is real. Most of us think of sin as being associated with drug use, too much liquor, and sleeping around and being involved with someone other than our spouse—but there are all kinds of sin. A negative attitude is sinful. A pessimistic mindset is sinful. Jealousy is sinful. Gossip is sinful. Guilt is sinful. The pursuit of pure, unadulterated pleasure, hedonism if you will, is sinful. Not giving God what is God's is sinful. Here it is. Sin promises enjoyment but in the end is an entrapment. We have all experienced sin as a trap. What starts out pleasurable and enjoyable eventually makes us slaves. We go someplace we never intended and stay longer than we anticipated.

The father embraces the son because he could have been destroyed emotionally or physically. What Scripture tells us is that the younger son squandered his inheritance on riotous living, in a contemporary context meaning street drugs and illegal substances and promiscuous sexual activity. He squandered his gifts and contaminated his soul. That kind of living could have left him with HIV, full-blown AIDS, or a number of other sexually transmitted diseases. The father recognized that his son could have been dead. But that was not the case. He was not in a hospital and he was not in a morgue. He comes home from a pigsty under the power of his remaining strength and he begs his father for forgiveness. And his father grants him that request.

God is truly a strong deliverer. Here's this young boy flashing money and his wealth in the streets. Somebody could have shot him or cut his throat, but the boy comes back alive and in his right mind. When we participate in behavior that can destroy us, we aren't in our right minds. Looking back over our lives, we will discover behavior that should have killed us but didn't because somebody prayed. Though my mother is dead, I believe her prayers are still in the atmosphere and encircle and protect me. She prayed that God would keep me, deliver me, heal me, and help me. Ultimately, like the prodigal son's father, she prayed that God would stop my dissipation before I was destroyed.

And so the father rejoices in the son's return: "My son, who was lost, is now found. My son, who was dead, is now alive." The son survived his experience and he survived near-dissipation and destruction. So there is in him something left to love. The father tells the elder son, "I see something else. I see in my found son a glowing and glaring transformation. He has made the journey from arrogance and superiority to humility. When he left home, he left saying, 'give me,' but now he has returned and he says, 'make me.' He said, 'Give me my share of the inheritance,' but now he comes back home and says, 'Make me one of your hired servants. I don't care whether I am a cook, a butler, or a stable boy. Anything's better than a pigpen attendant.'"

The prodigal son was born in a palace but ends up in a pigpen. Now a lot of us know what it's like to be a pigpen dweller, living with slop and hanging out with hogs. And some of us never return home. The prodigal son left home saying, "Give me," but he returns saying, "Make me." Pigpen servitude, living in the gutter, sometimes becomes the starting point for directing us where God would have us to go. The crucifixion comes before the resurrection. God gives us that resurrection. Sometimes God has to kill aspects of our attitude in order to develop our gratitude. Sometimes God has to destroy us before God can reconstruct us. Sometimes God has to make us kiss the nadir of the valley before we appreciate the summit of the mountain. Sometimes God has to make us cry out in order for us to appreciate laughter. "Lift up your heads, O you gates; lift them up, you ancient doors, that the King of glory may come in" (Psalm 24:9, NIV).

Now it was anathema that a Jew would place himself under the auspices of a Gentile master. During the time that Jesus walked the earth, Jews thought themselves to be ethnically superior to all Gentiles because Gentiles were considered pagans, and pagans were considered heathens. Although this young man had squandered everything he had and lived with pigs, but he stopped short of a slop mentality. It's one thing to get in mess, but it's quite another to live in mess. All of us have been in slop at some point, but we had enough sense not to stay there.

So here's a boy who's enjoined to a Gentile master and now he lives with pigs, which is against Jewish law and the Laws of Moses. He's reached rock bottom. The son realized that wealth—material, tangible prosperity—and even his "sonship" was not the goal this father had for him. The ultimate goal for all of us, regardless of what aim and ambition we have, is service. Jesus said, "The Son of Man did not come to be served, but to serve" (Matthew 20:28, NIV). Who is the greatest in the kingdom? The greatest is the one who serves. The marvel and wonder is what God will do, even when it comes to our mistakes, our missteps, and our mishaps—all of which are utilized in order to position and posture us for service.

When the Lord lets us scale great heights, it's all for the purpose of service. God wants us to take what God has given us and give back to somebody else. Whatever God has given—whether five talents, two talents, or one talent (see Matthew 25:15)—what we have been given is for the purpose of service. I am convinced that some of us can't handle success, and that many of us who achieve not only forget where we came from but look down on those who haven't had the same opportunities. God said, "I'll let you rise so that you can go back and help somebody else get to where I got you."

The prodigal son did not handle well the gifts of his birth. But even with his mistakes, there is always something left to love. There was a transformation from arrogance to humility. Notice in the text that the father embraces the younger son even though he was wasteful and rebellious, because he was never disrespectful. Rebellious, yes: "Give me my share of the inheritance," but disrespectful, no. When he's in pigpen slop, he still respects his father: "How many hired servants does my father have? I will arise, go to my father, and say to him, 'I am no more worthy to be called thy son; make me as one of your hired servants.'" He gives his father proper and respectful entitlement: "Father, I am no longer worthy. I'm ready now to relinquish my sonship if you'll just hire me as one of your servants." He rebelled against his father, but he never disrespected him.

We have different children at home today. Not only do they rebel, but they also disrespect. They feel entitled and it almost brings me to tears. It's not just that our children rebel and disappoint us. The prodigal son rebelled, and as parents we expect that, and the fictional character Walter Lee Younger from "A Raisin in the Sun" disappointed his family, but neither were disrespectful. Today, our children learn how to be disrespectful. They learn it in school, on the basketball court, and from all the electronic items we buy them. I don't worry about the hooded Klansman anymore when I walk the streets, but I am concerned for my safety when I encounter those whose rebellion and disrespect has led to the slop of violence. But even with them, there is something left to love.

In the Eastern world, old men never ran—never. They walked. But the text says that the father ran to meet the boy. He abandoned Eastern, Asian, Occidental culture because he loved his son. But there's more to it in Deuteronomy 21:18-21 (NIV): "If a man has a stubborn and rebellious son who does not obey his father and mother and will not listen to them when they discipline him, his father and mother shall take hold of him and bring him to the elders at the gate of this town. They shall say to the elders, 'This son of ours is stubborn and rebellious. He will not obey us. He is a profligate and a drunkard.' Then all the men of his town shall stone him to death. You must purge the evil from among you. All Israel will hear of it and be afraid."

So now we know why the father ran. Those in the village already knew that the young man had squandered his substance. The young man has already disgraced his mother and father and also shamed the whole town. So when he is seen coming home, the village folk can stone him. But the father runs and covers his once-lost son so that no one can harm him.

That's what Jesus does. When we mess up and stumble and fall and decide to return home, there might be those who want to stone us, but Jesus provides the covering and our Savior extends an arm of protection. When I messed up, when I stumbled and fell, there were folks who wanted to stone me. But my Savior ran interference and intercepted every stone. That's why I shout. That's why I can praise God. Jesus took a hit for the prodigal son and his jealous brother, and he even took the hit designed for me. Everybody has messed up and has done something shameful, but our Savior went up on a cross, shed His blood, and took a hit for your mistake and for mine.

The hymn writer says, "I once was lost, but now I'm found, was blind but now I see." Even though we lose our way sometimes, there is always something left to love. The parable about the prodigal son is ultimately about love and redemption and loving in and through storms. It is love that can save us. We've all been saved by grace, and grace is the price love pays. It doesn't matter where you were born or where you lived— Jesus took a hit for you because there is something good that remains. Jesus didn't have to do it, but He did. He took a hit for you because He said, "In you, there's always something left to love." Amen and Amen.

STRONGER IN MY BROKEN PLACES

Moses turned and went down the mountain with the two tablets of the Testimony in his hands. They were inscribed on both sides, front and back. The tablets were the work of God; the writing was the writing of God, engraved on the tablets. When Joshua heard the noise of the people shouting, he said to Moses, "There is the sound of war in the camp." Moses replied: "It is not the sound of victory, it is not the sound of defeat; it is the sound of singing that I hear." When Moses approached the camp and saw the calf and the dancing, his anger burned and he threw the tablets out of his hands, breaking them to pieces at the foot of the mountain. And he took the calf they had made and burned it in the fire; then he ground it to powder, scattered it on the water and made the Israelites drink it. . . . The next day Moses said to the people, "You have committed a great sin. But now I will go up to the LORD; perhaps I can make atonement for your sin." So Moses went back to the LORD and said, "Oh, what a great sin these people have committed! They have made themselves gods of gold. But now, please forgive their sin—but if not, then blot me out of the book you have written." The LORD replied to Moses, "Whoever has sinned against me I will blot out of my book. Now go, lead the people to the place I spoke of, and my angel will go before you. However, when the time comes for me to punish, I will punish them for their sin." And the LORD struck the people with a plague because of what they did with the calf Aaron had made. **Exodus 32:15-20, 30-35, NIV**

It would be an understatement to suggest that we live in a time when disappointments and setbacks occur on a regular basis. There has been for some time an errant theology afloat in the body of Christ that would have us believe that if we have sufficient faith we will not be victimized by disappointments, setbacks, sickness, and failures.

However, I would like to remind you of what are some of the stark realities of human existence which are applicable for saints and sinners alike. The reality is, we will experience dreadful disappointments. We will encounter shocking setbacks. We will have to deal with some toxic tension. And we will be forced to bounce back from some complicated calamities. The Bible says, the rain falls on the just and the unjust alike (Matthew 5:45).

Anybody who lives with the notion that he or she can dodge such bullets is not living in the real world. It is for this reason that a plethora of self-help books and tapes pertaining to psychology and psychiatry are now found upon bookcases within the average home. There are a large number of people who on a daily basis find themselves lying on a psychotherapist's couch in an attempt to deal with some heartache or heartbreak that has left them so disappointed that for them life is a very difficult pilgrimage to continue. Too many of us are ready to throw in the towel and concede to the pressures of life. People of every ethnicity are looking for assistance to make it from one day to the next.

One of the fastest-growing occupations in this culture is that of a "life coach." These individuals employ psychology, theology, and sociology in an attempt to assist people in their struggles. People of multiple professions and various pedigrees utilize these individuals to assist them with their perpetual problems and varying situations. I have nothing against the utilization of a life coach, but I still believe that the Word of God is "a lamp unto our feet and a light unto our path" (Psalm 119:105). I am a firm believer that Jesus is the ultimate "Life Coach" from whom the servants of God ought to acquire their coaching. It appears that many people view Jesus as less exciting than some of the more colorful personalities we see over the airwaves today.

It is no wonder that we have become such a personality and chemically dependent generation. In our insatiable need to feel attached to the ecstatic existence of this world, we are driven to seek out personalities that will allow us to live vicariously through them.

When I speak of personality dependency, I'm talking about the willingness of millions of consumers to purchase a book on the advice of a talk show host. Personality dependency occurs when you are willing to rush home from your place of employment on your limited lunch break to satisfy your daily addiction of your favorite television judge. Personality dependency seeks to ease a disappointment or self-defined deficiency in one's life. People are truly personality dependent when they can quote a person from television more than they can recite the Bible.

When I speak of chemical dependency, I'm not simply talking about illicit drugs. I'm also talking about prescribed drugs. Some of your most chemically dependent people are those who can afford to see a medical doctor and dispense big dollars for their legally prescribed medications. So many people require medication just to function on a daily basis. How many people have a difficult time living today without antidepressants? And how many people find it very difficult to maintain a healthy relationship with anybody without the aid of chemicals?

This difficulty goes beyond the traditional relationship between a man and a woman. Some of us have a difficult time with relationships when it comes to our parents or when it comes to our siblings. There aren't many drama-free functional families or individuals in our society; however, there are a lot of functioning dysfunctional families and individuals in our society. The emotional scars from our childhood run deep into the psyche of our existence. Few of us have platonic friends primarily because the emotional and psychological scars of previous encounters and relationships have left us emotionally and psychologically broken. If a person desires to move from a state of brokenness to a posture of strength and wholeness he or she must be willing to address and deal with the brokenness from their past. Brokenness leaves a trail that can be traced for others to follow. This is why a counselor will always have you discuss your feelings about your childhood and your parents. If you want to trace your brokenness, you must locate your unhealed hurts, identify your unmet needs, and confess your unresolved issues. An African proverb teaches us, "A concealed disease can never be healed."

Brokenness can invade your mind, spirit, and soul at any time in your life. Brokenness can occur by way of what we hear, by way of what we see, and by way of what we experience. It would appear that many of the issues that plague our lives have their roots in our childhood. This is not to suggest that brokenness never visits us in our later years—far from it. The evidence of our societal brokenness is played out every day with the dramatic increase—among young and old, black and white, blue-collar and white-collar people—of this insidious disease called suicide. There are people who have decided life has become so absurd that there is nothing worthwhile left in it at all, and they would rather kill themselves than face the possibility of a troubled future. They are disappointed, disturbed, distressed, and crippled to the point that death presents a better option than life. Many people echo the sentiments of Job's pain when he said, "I curse the day of my birth. May the day of my birth perish, and the night they said, a boy is born. I wish I was never born!" (Job 3:1-2).

There are multiple ways to address the hurt that has found residence in the soul. People deal with brokenness every day without the dependency of drugs. Black people have been dealing with the vicissitudes of life that should have annihilated us and left us broken beyond repair for years without the dependency of a human personality we thought should have been in our lives. Our women have raised strong sons and daughters, many without the assistance of a father. Our parents have worked hard and provided for their families for generations without the assistance of a just legal system. Our families have withstood the unfair practices of a people and a caste system that was hell bent on breaking our spirits, dashing our hopes, and crushing our dreams. We were not broken beyond repair then and we shall not be broken beyond repair now! How? We were able to survive because we kept our hands in the hand of the Lord. We kept our knees bent and our ears attuned to the directives of God.

One could safely make the argument that Moses should have been broken beyond repair. He was born in a country that wanted to kill him as a child; he was put in a basket upon the Nile River by his mother to escape persecution; he was raised in the household of the oppressor of his people; he was taught one thing by his mother, but exposed to another thing by the royal family during his formative years; he murdered a man when he saw the injustice against his people up close; he was forced to leave the comfort of the palace because of the information floating around town by the very people he was trying to help; he lived in the desert for forty years and then was told by God to return to a dark place he had run from. Moses was broken by sibling rivalry. Moses was broken by his longing to have a greater relationship with God. Moses was broken because he suffered from a lack of self-confidence. Nevertheless, with all of these broken pieces in his life, he decided to go forward with the challenge given to him.

While Moses was in the desert for forty years he underwent a metamorphosis from brokenness to wholeness. One must allow oneself to imagine the lessons that the Lord taught Moses by way of his involvement with nature, the daily farm duties of a shepherd, and the patience acquired by addressing the needs of some smelly sheep. One must allow oneself to imagine the talks Moses had with his father-in-law, Jethro, in the early dew of the morning and late into the dark nights. One must allow oneself to imagine the long walks and revealing conversations Moses shared with his wife, Zipporah.

There is something to be assumed about the movement of God's ability to insulate you after He has orchestrated the activities of your life to isolate you. Don't be afraid of going through a season of aloneness; God may be trying to help you deal with your brokenness. It is when you are in solitude that the spirit of God can adjust your attitude. Embrace your brokenness and remember that the contents of a vessel can't be utilized until the seal has been broken.

Since life can render us disappointing times, since life presents to us setbacks, what then can we do as God's servants in moving from brokenness to wholeness? What is that which can be lifted from the life of Moses that can help us deal and cope with the challenges of life? How can God use us as He heals us? Moses displays three things we can do to help us move from our brokenness to wholeness.

The first thing the text suggests we do to become stronger in our broken places is to be willing to serve as an intercessor between God and His people. Learning that the people had committed the dastardly sin of making themselves gods, Moses knew he had to serve as a go-between to help the people restore their covenantal relationship with God. Moses knew he had to help the people keep their eyes fixed upon the God of all creation and deliverance. Moses was broken when the Lord instructed him, "Go down, because your people, whom you brought up out of Egypt, have become corrupt" (Exodus 32:7).

Many times we become broken because of the things that we hear from God. Moses was broken because he had to break his communion with the Lord because of the actions of other people. Too often we allow the actions of others to break our communion with God. As Moses departed from the top of the mountain one can only imagine what was going through his psyche. Moses had to wonder how a people could willingly defy such a gracious God. Moses knows he will have to serve as God's spokesman and assist them in their understanding of who God actually is and what God has actually done for the people of Israel. It bothered him that the newly freed people, who had just recently agreed to keep the covenant with the Lord, quickly forgot Who brought them out of bondage.

How many of us are living in the midst of our brokenness because we decided to move away from God by breaking our personal agreements with God? Many people today aren't willing to have someone serve as an intercessor for them. However, as an intercessor, one must be willing to declare to the people what thus says the Lord.

In today's society many people need a liaison to remind them Who can deliver them from their brokenness and make them stronger from their experience. Many people insist on pushing their harsh realities underneath the proverbial rug of denial. Someone needs to serve as a third party between a person's pain and God's graciousness. One is not so spiritually self-sufficient that one doesn't need the assistance of others. None of us have it so all together that disappointments don't rock us sometimes and make us feel and wonder if we have a friend in heaven or on the earth. It is imperative for us to admit that sometimes we need to be reassured of the reality that there is a mighty God who sits high but looks low. God has gifted humanity with people in all walks of life to help us understand the mysteries of their existence.

Medical people in the world of anatomy and physiology teach and tell us that whenever a bone is broken and is properly set, its healing will allow the point of the break to be stronger than before. Please don't miss the truth of this anatomical illustration. The strongest point in your body is that place where you have experienced brokenness and God has allowed through the miracle of medicine and the miracle of His touch to heal and restore your breakage. Anybody who has broken an arm, broken a wrist, broken a leg, or broken an ankle can attest to the fact that at the healing point of the breakage emerged a greater strength. Therefore, a broken heart today has the potential to be a stronger heart tomorrow. A damaged mind today has the opportunity to be a stronger mind tomorrow. A bruised self-image today has the resiliency to become a stronger self-image tomorrow. A dysfunctional person today has the opportunity to become a functional person tomorrow. We are stronger in our broken places.

If this be true of the human body, if this is an anatomical and physiological axiom, then it must also be true spiritually. At the place I break, if I allow the Holy Spirit to reset the breakage, I don't have to fall apart at the seams. I don't have to go around as if I'm somebody without hope because the point where I am broken—if I allow God to heal the wound—becomes the point of my strength. We are stronger in our broken places.

The church ought to be a place where the broken have a chance to be made whole. All too often a person who claims to be a Christian gives God a black eye and the church a bad name because he or she doesn't know how to handle his or her breakage. As we see here in the text many of the people had a difficult time waiting on Moses to return from the Lord. Many people like to regress to some of their old habits to help them deal with their brokenness. You don't have to handle your brokenness with drugs, alcohol, or with sexual promiscuity. I understand everyone falls short of the glory of God, but as a Christian one ought to acknowledge that God strengthened you at the point of your brokenness. Your brokenness becomes your testimony. Your brokenness becomes your credential that allows you to encourage someone else of God's power and might.

Moses had to address his brokenness based on what he heard from God before he could adequately address the brokenness of the people. Although broken by the behavior of the people, Moses understood that he had to allow God to use him to get the people back on course with God and in alignment with the will of God. He understood that the people had to learn how to wait and trust the movement of God. Moses understood that a mangled people today have the power, with the grace of God, to become a stronger people tomorrow.

Moses is broken because of what he heard from God, but he becomes even more broken because of what he sees the people actually doing. He sees a people who have truly disrespected their God and committed a deadly sin. Moses loses it and he breaks the tablets. He smashes them on the ground. Then he looks at the idol and throws it into the fire. He grinds the powder from the ashes, sprinkles it in the water, and instructs the people to drink their own ideology. Moses is really disappointed by their act of debauchery and immorality. Nevertheless, he understands that despite his feelings he must allow himself to edify the people. One way God helps us transition from our broken state is by using us to assist others in their brokenness. We all must learn to deal with our hurt while seeking to help others. One cannot give up or give in to their pain and disappointments while attempting to enlighten others.

The second thing that Moses teaches is we should define ourselves more by our disappointments than by our dreams. More strength came forth from Moses' disappointments than from his dreams. The same is the case for us. The reason that I come to this is because, in most instances, one has more disappointments in life than dreams. Some of our dreams are on hold. Some of our dreams will never materialize. We are defined more by our disappointments than we are by our dreams. It is in the trials of life that authentic character gets a chance to reveal itself.

It was never the dream of Moses to become Israel's liberator. It was never the dream of Moses to go before Pharaoh and challenge his rule. His dream was to become a prince and remain in all of grandeur that Egypt had to offer him as an Egyptian prince. That was Moses' dream. But that wasn't God's dream. God can be annoying by quietly converting our dreams and allowing us to live within what appears to be disappointing situations in order to bring His plan to pass in our lives.

Jochebed, Moses' mother, had been taken to Pharaoh's daughter by Miriam. It was Jochebed who actually nursed Moses, and she nursed him by reciting in his hearing the history of his people. One day at 40 years old, Moses goes to Goshen, which is the Jewish ghetto, and he witnesses an Egyptian beating a Hebrew. He can't take it. His rage rises, violence takes over, and he kills the Egyptian and buries his body in the sand. He becomes a murderer. He never dreamed of becoming that. Then he runs and he becomes a fugitive from justice. And for the next forty years of his life, he lives in the desert of Midian. He meets Jethro, the priest, who becomes his father-in-law and his counselor. He marries and has children. So now he's living out in the desert—that's a long way from the palace. Some may define his life as disappointed. One thing is for sure—it wasn't a part of his dream for his life.

Then God calls him. Now God can be annoying. I mean, God is the kind of deity who will add insult to injury. Moses is not a prince anymore. He's living out in the desert. He's married, has all these kids, and then God says, "I want you to go back and inform Pharaoh that I'm going to pull the rug out from under his economy and take the slave population and lead them into the land of promise."

Moses is not molded by his dreams. Moses is molded by his disappointments. For the young and old alike who are trying to put their lives back together again because of some dream that has yet to come true, stay strong in the Lord. Accept that when the Lord allows disappointment to happen, it means there's something in the disappointment that He is trying to get you to see. Disappointment must be redefined when looked at through the lenses of God.

Some of you have been looking at this thing totally wrong. You want to look at every disappointment as being from the Devil. You want to think that every setback comes from the adversary. No. Some of this stuff comes from God. I know you don't want to believe it, but God will sometimes make you go through hell to really appreciate Him. Sometimes He'll make you cry so that you can really laugh about something. How can you appreciate the mountain if you haven't walked through the valley? How can you appreciate the sunshine if you haven't been in the rain and in the clouds? Disappointments ultimately are not millstones; they are stepping stones.

You must learn how to recycle disappointment. You must be willing to grapple with the issues of life and learn to depend on God for guidance through your rough times. Disappointments can help you develop your devotional time with God. It can help you develop purposeful prayer life. It is in your disappointments that you are encouraged to develop a more consistent Bible study ritual. You're not defined by your dreams; you are defined by your disappointments. As Booker T. Washington said, "Success is not measured by the position one has reached in life, rather the obstacles overcome while trying to succeed."

I have always been enraptured with Alex Haley's *Roots*—not just with *Roots*, but with the sequel *Roots: The Next Generation*. What a marvelous story of one man's family. The story of Alex Haley's family is your story and mine. All of the authenticity of our inner strength can be traced back to Kunta Kinte. Look at the story and how he was brought to this country after being snatched out of a Gambian jungle while going out to look for wood in order to make something. The dream was that he would be forever successful in that village. But he was captured by slave traders, taken across the watery deep of the Atlantic, survived the Middle Passage, and brought here to this land called America, where they cut off his foot and finally succeeded to change his name from Kunta Kinte to Toby.

Roots is the story of a lineage that defines disappointment in the context of stepping stones and not millstones. Alex Haley tried to live in his father's dream. However, he was unsuccessful in his efforts. Many people are living challenging lives trying to live their parents' dream. God never told you to live their dream. You have to live your own dreams.

Simon Haley wanted Alex to be a college graduate, but Alex wanted to be a writer. He dropped out of college and joined the Coast Guard.

While in the Coast Guard, against his father's wishes, he married and had children. The marriage fell apart and he and his wife divorced, but he kept pursuing his own dream. He co-wrote *The Autobiography of Malcolm X* with Malcolm X. He wrote to his father on the inside of an autographed copy, "I no longer need your approval, but I'll always need your love." He went on to write *Roots* and to become one of the most prolific writers in our generation. He would have never become that if he had viewed his disappointments as a millstone. He became stronger in his place of brokenness. He was stronger because he understood that his disappointments made him the person who he was meant to be at the insistence of God.

Who does God want you to be? Are you willing to accept the plans of God for your life as He reveals them to you? Saul of Tarsus wanted to be a great rabbi like Gamaliel, but that isn't who God wanted him to be. God wanted him to become Paul the Apostle to the Gentiles in Asia Minor.

Nelson Mandela wanted to be a lawyer, but God had another plan. He wanted him to be locked up for twenty-seven years, so that he could eventually become the first Black president of South Africa.

Martin Luther King, Jr. had a dream of succeeding Benjamin Mays as the President of Morehouse College. That was his dream. God had another dream for him—to be our Black Moses who would go up against segregation and discrimination.

Who does God want you to be? Maybe you're struggling in your life because you have not properly defined your disappointment. Are still kicking trying to live out a dream that God never intended for you?

Moses dreamed of becoming a prince, but God meant for him to become a liberator. Moses dreamed of giving instructions to slaves, as a prince, but God wanted him to become an instructor of the slaves, as a prophet. It did not matter that he was raised in Egyptian culture. It did not matter that he spoke Hebrew with an Egyptian accent. It did not matter that he was even a murderer. Disappointments afforded Moses the opportunity to develop an outer shell of tough skin and an inner layer of assurance of God's power.

Moses teaches us that our disappointments help make us the people who God means for us to be, and not the person we dream of becoming. Whatever your hurts, whatever your pains, whatever your setbacks, and whatever your disappointments, they can never take away the last of your human freedoms as you move from brokenness to wholeness.

The final thing that Moses teaches us to do as we move from our brokenness to our strength is to exercise our right to choose what our attitude will be in any given circumstance. Moses says to the people, "You have committed a great sin. But now I will go up to the Lord; perhaps I can make atonement for you sins." It doesn't matter what has happened to you; you still have an option of the attitude you will have towards that incident. You are free to respond to the pain as you choose to do so. Typically, people respond to their brokenness in one of two ways. You can either let the pain control you or you can control the pain. In either case, you've got to make an attitude adjustment. You have to learn how to roll with the punches of life and display an attitude of a victor and not that of a victim. Benjamin Mays once said, "To be able to stand the troubles of life, one must have a sense of mission and a belief that God sent him or her into the world for a purpose, to do something unique and distinctive; and if he or she does not do it, life will be worse off because it was not done."

All of us must make the conscious decision to succeed in life by making the decision not to fail in life. One can either allow their peril to break them or build them. In the end, it is imperative for all of us to take the responsibility for our own destiny as we rely on the activities of God in our lives. When travail visits you and you start to feel gloomy, step back and encourage yourself by acknowledging that you need an attitude adjustment.

In a heavyweight championship fight between Mike Tyson and a little-known fighter named Buster Douglas a few years ago, Douglas was knocked down and it appeared that Iron Mike had assaulted another victim in the boxing ring. However, on this day Douglas was fighting for more than a title belt. He was fighting for the pride and honor of his recently deceased mother. His strength was both physical and spiritual. In the deepest corridors of his existence was the battle cry of his mother, "You can do it." Douglas had to choose to stay down or get up. Not only did he get up, he went on to knock out the supposedly invincible heavyweight champion of the world.

Moses had a choice: stay mad and angry or adopt the nature of his Creator. Too many people allow themselves to stay down on the canvas of life. Moses had spent forty years in the desert with people who probably taught him how to appreciate life for what it is and not for what he felt it should have been. It is plausible that Jethro, his father-in-law, could have taught him another side of God that was slightly different from his Egyptian rearing. God still has good folk in many places who can help you learn things about God that will enhance your attitude towards Him and your views toward your disappointments. God still has open doors that no man can shut. Don't allow yourself to be surrounded with people who specialize in toxic testimonies of the mundane. They are poisoning your attitude. You have to surround yourself with some people who can feed you a healthy dose of "you can make it" affirmations. You have to believe that you can rise above whatever or whoever is trying to break you.

Moses could have stayed angry; he could have stayed bitter. But instead he decided to adopt the nature of his Creator. He went to God and dialectally he presented a thesis: "Now Lord, if you have to blot out anybody, blot me out. The people have sinned. There isn't any doubt about that. But I want mercy for the people. When I look back over my life, I see is empathy, I see compassion, I see grace. It started out when I was born, when Pharaoh was committing genocide and killing all Hebrew male children. I survived the Nile and ended up in the enemy's bathing pool, and the oppressor had to raise the liberator. Then I killed that Egyptian one day and buried his body in the sand. But you gave me another chance—grace. So I want you to forgive their sin. They're wrong. They should have never fashioned the image of the golden calf. They should have never gotten involved in debauchery and immorality. But if you can put it on me and let them live, that will be all right."

But God said, "That's all right. I hear what you're saying. But they are going to pay for what they did." In my spiritual imagination I can hear God telling Moses, "What they did was not an affront to you, but to me. But I'll tell you what, my servant, although you can't atone for their sin, I will allow you to be an ambassador and lead them to the promised land of milk and honey because you have made an attitude adjustment towards the people. And Moses, relax, I already have Somebody who's waiting in the wings of time who will be a suitable atonement for the sin of people. It isn't His time yet. One day, in the fullness of time, I'm going to send my Son, who's going to tiptoe down the stairway of heaven to atone for sin." It is imperative to know that Moses was not an acceptable atonement for the people of Israel. However, he was an acceptable vessel to serve as liberator for the people of Israel on behalf of God.

Moses could have chosen to stay in his brokenness, but he was willing to serve as an intercessor between God and His people. More strength came forth from Moses' disappointments than from his dreams. He chose what his attitude would be in circumstances. As in the time of Moses, we live in a time when disappointments and setbacks occur on a regular basis, but like Moses, we are stronger in our broken places. I want to encourage you to shout: I am stronger in my broken places!